50 Premium Restaurant Cooking Recipes for Home

By: Kelly Johnson

Table of Contents

- Lobster Bisque
- Beef Wellington
- Truffle Risotto
- Duck à l'Orange
- Tuna Tartare
- Lobster Mac and Cheese
- Osso Buco
- Foie Gras Torchon
- Black Truffle Pasta
- Pan-Seared Scallops
- Rack of Lamb with Mint Pesto
- Lobster Ravioli
- Lobster Thermidor
- Beef Bourguignon
- Chilean Sea Bass
- Chateaubriand Steak
- Coq au Vin
- Peking Duck
- Duck Confit
- Bouillabaisse
- Veal Osso Buco
- Salmon en Papillote
- Filet Mignon
- Beef Tenderloin with Red Wine Sauce
- Moroccan Tagine
- Braised Short Ribs
- Lobster Newberg
- Roasted Bone Marrow
- Foie Gras Burger
- Wild Mushroom Risotto
- Beef Stroganoff
- Sautéed Foie Gras with Apple Compote

- Crab Cakes with Remoulade
- Pan-Roasted Veal Chop
- Stuffed Poblano Peppers
- Sweetbreads with Capers
- Ahi Tuna with Soy Ginger Glaze
- Beef Carpaccio
- Seafood Paella
- Tuna Poke Bowl
- Roasted Cornish Hen
- Miso-Glazed Black Cod
- Grilled Lobster Tail
- Braised Lamb Shanks
- Butternut Squash Soup
- Pork Belly with Apple Chutney
- Crispy Duck Breast
- Baked Alaska
- Chocolate Fondant
- Classic Tiramisu

Lobster Bisque

Ingredients:

- 2 live lobsters (about 1 1/2 lbs each)
- 2 tbsp butter
- 1 onion, finely chopped
- 2 celery stalks, finely chopped
- 1 carrot, finely chopped
- 3 garlic cloves, minced
- 1/4 cup tomato paste
- 1/2 cup dry white wine
- 4 cups seafood stock (or chicken broth)
- 1 cup heavy cream
- 1 tbsp brandy (optional)
- 1 bay leaf
- 1/4 tsp cayenne pepper (optional, for heat)
- 1/2 tsp paprika
- Salt and freshly ground black pepper, to taste
- Fresh parsley, chopped (for garnish)
- Lobster meat (from the cooked lobsters), chopped

Instructions:

1. **Cook the Lobster:**
    - Bring a large pot of salted water to a boil. Add the lobsters and cook for 8-10 minutes, until the shells turn bright red. Remove the lobsters and let them cool.
    - Once cool, remove the meat from the shells and set aside. Save the shells for making the stock.
2. **Make the Stock:**
    - In a large pot, add a bit of water and the lobster shells. Simmer for about 30 minutes, then strain and set aside.
3. **Prepare the Bisque Base:**
    - In a large pot, melt the butter over medium heat. Add the onion, celery, and carrot, and cook until softened, about 5-7 minutes.
    - Add the garlic and cook for another minute.
    - Stir in the tomato paste and cook for 2 minutes.
    - Deglaze the pot with the white wine, scraping up any bits from the bottom. Cook until the wine is reduced by half.
4. **Simmer and Blend:**
    - Add the seafood stock (or chicken broth), bay leaf, paprika, and cayenne pepper if using. Bring to a simmer and cook for 20 minutes.

- Remove the bay leaf. Use an immersion blender to puree the soup until smooth. (Alternatively, blend in batches using a regular blender.)
5. **Finish the Bisque:**
    - Return the bisque to the heat. Stir in the heavy cream and brandy, if using. Simmer gently for another 10 minutes, adjusting seasoning with salt and pepper to taste.
    - Add the chopped lobster meat and cook until heated through.
6. **Serve:**
    - Ladle the bisque into bowls and garnish with chopped parsley.

This Lobster Bisque is rich, creamy, and full of luxurious lobster flavor, perfect for a special occasion or a fancy dinner at home.

Beef Wellington

Ingredients:

For the Beef:

- 2 lb beef tenderloin (center-cut)
- Olive oil
- Salt and freshly ground black pepper
- 2 tbsp Dijon mustard

For the Duxelles:

- 2 tbsp unsalted butter
- 1 small onion, finely chopped
- 2 garlic cloves, minced
- 12 oz cremini or button mushrooms, finely chopped
- 1/4 cup dry white wine
- Salt and freshly ground black pepper
- 1 tbsp fresh thyme leaves

For Assembly:

- 8 slices prosciutto
- 1 sheet puff pastry (thawed if frozen)
- 1 egg, beaten (for egg wash)
- 1 tbsp flour (for dusting)

Instructions:

1. **Prepare the Beef:**
    - Preheat your oven to 400°F (200°C).
    - Season the beef tenderloin generously with salt and pepper. Heat olive oil in a large skillet over high heat. Sear the beef on all sides until browned (about 2-3 minutes per side). Remove from heat and let cool.
    - Brush the beef with Dijon mustard and set aside.
2. **Prepare the Duxelles:**
    - In the same skillet, melt butter over medium heat. Add the onion and garlic and cook until softened (about 5 minutes).
    - Add the finely chopped mushrooms and cook until the liquid evaporates and the mixture becomes dry (about 10 minutes).
    - Stir in the white wine and cook until evaporated. Add thyme, salt, and pepper. Remove from heat and let cool.
3. **Assemble the Wellington:**

- Lay out a large sheet of plastic wrap. Arrange the prosciutto slices in an overlapping pattern on the plastic wrap. Spread the mushroom duxelles evenly over the prosciutto.
- Place the beef on top of the duxelles. Using the plastic wrap, roll the prosciutto and mushrooms around the beef tightly. Chill in the refrigerator for about 15 minutes.

4. **Wrap in Puff Pastry:**
    - Roll out the puff pastry on a floured surface to a rectangle large enough to cover the beef. Remove the plastic wrap from the beef.
    - Place the beef in the center of the puff pastry. Fold the pastry over the beef, sealing the edges by pinching them together. Brush the edges with beaten egg to seal.
    - Place the wrapped beef seam-side down on a baking sheet lined with parchment paper. Brush the entire surface with beaten egg.

5. **Bake:**
    - Bake in the preheated oven for 25-30 minutes, or until the puff pastry is golden brown and the internal temperature of the beef reaches 125°F (52°C) for medium-rare.
    - Let the Wellington rest for 10 minutes before slicing.

6. **Serve:**
    - Slice and serve with your favorite sides, such as roasted vegetables or a rich red wine sauce.

Beef Wellington is a show-stopping dish with tender beef wrapped in a layer of savory mushrooms and crisp puff pastry, perfect for special occasions.

Truffle Risotto

Ingredients:

- 1 cup Arborio rice
- 1 small onion, finely chopped
- 2 garlic cloves, minced
- 4 cups chicken or vegetable broth (hot)
- 1 cup dry white wine
- 2 tbsp unsalted butter
- 2 tbsp olive oil
- 1/2 cup freshly grated Parmesan cheese
- 2-3 tbsp truffle oil (adjust to taste)
- 1 small black truffle (optional, thinly shaved, for garnish)
- Salt and freshly ground black pepper, to taste
- Fresh parsley, chopped (for garnish)

Instructions:

1. **Prepare the Broth:**
    - Keep the chicken or vegetable broth warm in a saucepan over low heat.
2. **Sauté Aromatics:**
    - In a large skillet or saucepan, heat the olive oil and 1 tablespoon of butter over medium heat.
    - Add the chopped onion and cook until softened and translucent (about 5 minutes).
    - Stir in the minced garlic and cook for another 1-2 minutes, until fragrant.
3. **Toast the Rice:**
    - Add the Arborio rice to the skillet. Stir well to coat the rice with the oil and butter.
    - Cook for 2-3 minutes, until the edges of the rice become translucent and slightly toasted.
4. **Deglaze with Wine:**
    - Pour in the white wine, stirring constantly, until the wine is fully absorbed by the rice.
5. **Add Broth Gradually:**
    - Begin adding the hot broth to the rice, one ladleful at a time. Stir frequently and let the rice absorb the liquid before adding more.
    - Continue this process until the rice is creamy and tender, but still has a slight bite to it (about 18-20 minutes).
6. **Finish the Risotto:**
    - Stir in the remaining 1 tablespoon of butter and the freshly grated Parmesan cheese.
    - Drizzle the truffle oil over the risotto and stir gently to combine. Season with salt and pepper to taste.

7. **Serve:**
    - Spoon the risotto onto plates or into bowls.
    - Garnish with thinly shaved black truffle, if using, and a sprinkle of fresh parsley.
8. **Enjoy:**
    - Serve immediately for the best texture and flavor.

Truffle Risotto is a luxurious and creamy dish that combines the rich, earthy aroma of truffles with the comforting texture of Arborio rice, making it a perfect choice for special occasions or a sophisticated weeknight dinner.

Duck à l'Orange

Ingredients:

For the Duck:

- 1 whole duck (about 5-6 lbs)
- Salt and freshly ground black pepper
- 1 orange, quartered
- 1 onion, quartered
- 2 garlic cloves, crushed

For the Orange Sauce:

- 1 cup fresh orange juice
- 1/2 cup chicken broth
- 1/4 cup white wine
- 2 tbsp sugar
- 2 tbsp white wine vinegar
- 2 tbsp cornstarch mixed with 2 tbsp cold water (for thickening)
- 1 tbsp unsalted butter
- 1 tbsp finely grated orange zest
- Salt and freshly ground black pepper, to taste

Instructions:

1. **Prepare the Duck:**
    - Preheat your oven to 350°F (175°C).
    - Remove any excess fat from the duck and pat it dry with paper towels.
    - Season the duck generously with salt and pepper inside and out.
    - Stuff the cavity with the quartered orange, onion, and crushed garlic.
    - Truss the duck legs with kitchen twine and tuck the wings under the bird.
2. **Roast the Duck:**
    - Place the duck on a rack in a roasting pan, breast side up.
    - Roast in the preheated oven for about 2 to 2 1/2 hours, or until the skin is crisp and the internal temperature of the duck reaches 165°F (74°C).
    - Baste occasionally with its own juices to ensure even cooking and crisp skin.
3. **Prepare the Orange Sauce:**
    - While the duck is roasting, combine the orange juice, chicken broth, white wine, and sugar in a saucepan.
    - Bring to a simmer over medium heat and cook until reduced by half.
    - Stir in the white wine vinegar and cook for another 5 minutes.
    - Mix the cornstarch with cold water and stir it into the sauce. Cook until the sauce thickens.

- Remove from heat and stir in the butter and orange zest. Season with salt and pepper to taste.
4. **Finish and Serve:**
    - Once the duck is done, remove it from the oven and let it rest for about 15 minutes before carving.
    - Strain the duck drippings and add them to the orange sauce for extra flavor, if desired.
    - Carve the duck and serve it with the orange sauce spooned over the top.

Duck à l'Orange is a timeless French classic that pairs tender, succulent duck with a tangy and sweet orange sauce, creating a perfect balance of flavors for a special meal.

Tuna Tartare

Ingredients:

- 1/2 lb fresh sushi-grade tuna, finely diced
- 1 avocado, finely diced
- 2 tbsp soy sauce
- 1 tbsp sesame oil
- 1 tbsp lime juice
- 1 tsp finely grated ginger
- 1 small shallot, finely minced
- 1 tbsp capers, chopped
- 1 tbsp fresh cilantro, chopped
- 1/2 tsp sriracha or to taste (optional, for heat)
- Salt and freshly ground black pepper, to taste
- Thinly sliced radishes or cucumber (for garnish)
- Microgreens or additional cilantro (for garnish)
- Tortilla chips or wonton crisps (for serving)

Instructions:

1. **Prepare Tuna and Avocado:**
   - Dice the sushi-grade tuna into small cubes and place in a mixing bowl.
   - Dice the avocado and add it to the bowl with the tuna.
2. **Mix the Dressing:**
   - In a small bowl, whisk together the soy sauce, sesame oil, lime juice, grated ginger, and minced shallot.
3. **Combine Ingredients:**
   - Pour the dressing over the tuna and avocado mixture. Gently toss to combine without mashing the avocado.
4. **Add Additional Ingredients:**
   - Stir in the chopped capers, cilantro, and sriracha if using. Adjust seasoning with salt and pepper to taste.
5. **Plate and Garnish:**
   - Using a ring mold or by carefully spooning, plate the tartare mixture on serving plates.
   - Garnish with thinly sliced radishes or cucumber and a few microgreens or additional cilantro.
6. **Serve:**
   - Serve immediately with tortilla chips or wonton crisps on the side.

Tuna Tartare is a sophisticated and fresh appetizer that combines tender tuna with creamy avocado and a flavorful dressing, perfect for a special occasion or as a refreshing starter.

Lobster Mac and Cheese

Ingredients:

For the Mac and Cheese:

- 1 lb elbow macaroni or cavatappi
- 2 tbsp unsalted butter
- 2 tbsp all-purpose flour
- 2 cups whole milk
- 1 cup heavy cream
- 2 cups shredded sharp cheddar cheese
- 1 cup shredded Gruyère cheese
- 1/2 cup grated Parmesan cheese
- 1/2 tsp paprika
- 1/4 tsp cayenne pepper (optional, for a bit of heat)
- Salt and freshly ground black pepper, to taste
- 1 cup cooked lobster meat, chopped

For the Topping:

- 1/2 cup panko breadcrumbs
- 2 tbsp unsalted butter, melted
- 1/4 cup grated Parmesan cheese

Instructions:

1. **Cook the Pasta:**
    - Cook the macaroni or cavatappi in a large pot of salted boiling water according to package instructions until al dente. Drain and set aside.
2. **Make the Cheese Sauce:**
    - In a large saucepan, melt 2 tablespoons of butter over medium heat. Stir in the flour and cook for 1-2 minutes to form a roux.
    - Gradually whisk in the milk and heavy cream. Continue to whisk until the mixture is smooth and begins to thicken.
    - Reduce the heat to low and stir in the shredded cheddar, Gruyère, and Parmesan cheeses. Continue stirring until the cheeses are fully melted and the sauce is smooth.
    - Season with paprika, cayenne pepper (if using), salt, and pepper to taste.
3. **Combine Pasta and Lobster:**
    - Gently fold the cooked pasta and chopped lobster meat into the cheese sauce until well combined.
4. **Prepare the Topping:**

    - In a small bowl, mix the panko breadcrumbs with melted butter and grated Parmesan cheese.
5. **Bake:**
    - Preheat your oven to 375°F (190°C).
    - Transfer the mac and cheese mixture to a baking dish. Sprinkle the breadcrumb topping evenly over the top.
    - Bake in the preheated oven for 25-30 minutes, or until the top is golden brown and the sauce is bubbling.
6. **Serve:**
    - Let the Lobster Mac and Cheese cool for a few minutes before serving.

This Lobster Mac and Cheese combines the creamy, cheesy goodness of classic mac and cheese with succulent lobster meat, creating a luxurious and satisfying dish that's perfect for special occasions or a comforting treat.

Osso Buco

Ingredients:

- 4 veal shanks (about 1 1/2 inches thick)
- Salt and freshly ground black pepper
- 1/4 cup all-purpose flour
- 2 tbsp olive oil
- 2 tbsp unsalted butter
- 1 onion, finely chopped
- 2 carrots, finely chopped
- 2 celery stalks, finely chopped
- 4 garlic cloves, minced
- 1 cup dry white wine
- 1 can (14.5 oz) diced tomatoes
- 2 cups beef or chicken broth
- 1 cup fresh parsley, chopped
- 1 lemon, zested
- 1 tsp dried thyme
- 2 bay leaves
- 1 tbsp tomato paste

For the Gremolata:

- 1/4 cup fresh parsley, chopped
- 1 garlic clove, minced
- 1 tbsp lemon zest

Instructions:

1. **Prepare the Shanks:**
   - Preheat your oven to 350°F (175°C).
   - Season the veal shanks with salt and pepper, then dredge in flour, shaking off any excess.
2. **Brown the Shanks:**
   - In a large Dutch oven or heavy ovenproof pot, heat the olive oil and butter over medium-high heat.
   - Add the veal shanks and brown on all sides, about 4-5 minutes per side. Remove the shanks and set aside.
3. **Sauté the Vegetables:**
   - In the same pot, add the onion, carrots, and celery. Cook until softened, about 8 minutes.
   - Stir in the garlic and cook for another minute.
4. **Deglaze and Simmer:**

- Pour in the white wine, scraping up any browned bits from the bottom of the pot. Cook until the wine is reduced by half.
- Stir in the diced tomatoes, beef broth, tomato paste, thyme, and bay leaves.

5. **Cook the Osso Buco:**
   - Return the veal shanks to the pot, nestling them into the sauce.
   - Cover the pot and transfer to the preheated oven. Bake for 1 1/2 to 2 hours, or until the meat is tender and falls off the bone.

6. **Prepare the Gremolata:**
   - While the osso buco is cooking, mix together the parsley, garlic, and lemon zest in a small bowl. Set aside.

7. **Finish and Serve:**
   - Remove the veal shanks from the pot and discard the bay leaves.
   - Skim any excess fat from the sauce, then stir in the chopped parsley and lemon zest.
   - Serve the osso buco with the sauce spooned over the top, and garnish with gremolata.

Osso Buco is a classic Italian dish featuring tender veal shanks braised in a rich tomato and wine sauce, finished with a fresh gremolata for added brightness and flavor. It's perfect served over risotto or polenta.

Foie Gras Torchon

Ingredients:

- 1 whole foie gras (about 1 lb), deveined
- 1/2 cup cognac or Armagnac
- 1/2 cup heavy cream
- 1/4 cup milk
- 1/4 cup sugar
- 1 tsp salt
- 1/2 tsp white pepper
- 1/2 tsp pink curing salt (optional, for color)
- 2 tbsp finely chopped fresh thyme or other herbs (optional)

Instructions:

1. **Prepare the Foie Gras:**
   - Gently separate the foie gras lobes and remove any visible veins. If not already done, devein the foie gras by carefully pulling out the veins with your fingers or using a small knife.
2. **Marinate:**
   - Place the foie gras in a bowl and pour over the cognac or Armagnac. Add the salt, sugar, white pepper, and optional pink curing salt. Mix well and let marinate in the refrigerator for at least 4 hours, or overnight for best results.
3. **Prepare the Mixture:**
   - After marinating, drain the foie gras from the cognac mixture and place it in a blender or food processor. Add the heavy cream and milk. Blend until very smooth, then pass the mixture through a fine sieve to ensure a silky texture.
4. **Prepare the Torchons:**
   - Lay out a clean kitchen towel or cheesecloth. Place the foie gras mixture in the center, then fold the cloth around the mixture to form a tight log shape. Tie the ends securely with kitchen twine, ensuring there are no air bubbles.
5. **Cook the Torchon:**
   - Fill a large pot with water and bring to a simmer. Submerge the foie gras torchons in the simmering water and cook gently for 20-25 minutes, maintaining a temperature of around 160°F (70°C). Use a thermometer to ensure precise cooking.
6. **Chill and Set:**
   - Remove the torchons from the water and let them cool slightly. Refrigerate for at least 6 hours, or preferably overnight, to fully set.
7. **Serve:**
   - To serve, unwrap the foie gras torchon from the cloth and slice into rounds. Serve with toasted brioche or crusty bread, and accompany with a fruit chutney or pickled vegetables.

Foie Gras Torchon is a luxurious and elegant appetizer, perfect for special occasions. The smooth, rich texture of the foie gras paired with a hint of cognac creates a memorable culinary experience.

Black Truffle Pasta

Ingredients:

- 8 oz pasta (tagliatelle, fettuccine, or pappardelle work well)
- 2 tbsp unsalted butter
- 2 tbsp olive oil
- 1 small shallot, finely chopped
- 2 garlic cloves, minced
- 1 cup heavy cream
- 1/2 cup freshly grated Parmesan cheese
- 1-2 tbsp black truffle oil (to taste)
- 1 small black truffle, thinly shaved (optional, for garnish)
- Salt and freshly ground black pepper, to taste
- Fresh parsley, chopped (for garnish)

Instructions:

1. **Cook the Pasta:**
     - Cook the pasta in a large pot of salted boiling water according to package instructions until al dente. Reserve 1/2 cup of pasta water, then drain and set aside.
2. **Prepare the Sauce:**
     - In a large skillet, heat the butter and olive oil over medium heat. Add the chopped shallot and cook until softened, about 3-4 minutes.
     - Stir in the minced garlic and cook for an additional minute, until fragrant.
     - Pour in the heavy cream and bring to a simmer. Cook until the cream slightly thickens, about 5 minutes.
3. **Combine Ingredients:**
     - Add the grated Parmesan cheese to the cream sauce, stirring until melted and smooth.
     - Stir in the black truffle oil and season with salt and pepper to taste.
4. **Toss the Pasta:**
     - Add the cooked pasta to the skillet with the sauce, tossing to coat the pasta evenly. If the sauce is too thick, add a bit of the reserved pasta water to reach the desired consistency.
5. **Serve:**
     - Transfer the pasta to serving plates. Garnish with thinly shaved black truffle, if using, and a sprinkle of chopped parsley.
6. **Enjoy:**
     - Serve immediately for the best flavor and texture.

Black Truffle Pasta is a luxurious dish that combines creamy, rich sauce with the earthy aroma of black truffles, creating an indulgent meal that's perfect for special occasions or a gourmet treat.

Pan-Seared Scallops

Ingredients:

- 1 lb large sea scallops (about 12-16)
- Salt and freshly ground black pepper
- 2 tbsp olive oil or unsalted butter
- 2 tbsp unsalted butter (if using olive oil for searing)
- 2 garlic cloves, minced
- 1 tbsp fresh lemon juice
- Fresh parsley or chives, chopped (for garnish)
- Lemon wedges (for serving)

Instructions:

1. **Prepare the Scallops:**
    - Pat the scallops dry with paper towels. Remove the side muscle (a small, tough piece on the side) if it hasn't already been removed.
    - Season the scallops generously with salt and freshly ground black pepper.
2. **Heat the Pan:**
    - Heat a large skillet over medium-high heat. Add the olive oil or half of the butter and let it heat until shimmering (but not smoking).
3. **Sear the Scallops:**
    - Place the scallops in the hot pan, making sure they are not overcrowded. Sear them without moving them for 2-3 minutes on one side, until a golden-brown crust forms.
    - Flip the scallops carefully and add the remaining butter to the pan. Sear for an additional 1-2 minutes on the other side, until the scallops are opaque in the center and have a golden crust.
4. **Add Garlic and Lemon:**
    - Add the minced garlic to the pan and cook for 30 seconds, just until fragrant. Be careful not to burn the garlic.
    - Deglaze the pan with the lemon juice, scraping up any browned bits from the bottom of the pan. Swirl the scallops in the pan to coat with the lemony butter sauce.
5. **Serve:**
    - Transfer the scallops to plates or a serving platter. Spoon the garlic-lemon butter sauce over the scallops.
    - Garnish with chopped parsley or chives and serve with lemon wedges on the side.
6. **Enjoy:**
    - Serve immediately with your choice of side dishes, such as a light salad, risotto, or roasted vegetables.

Pan-Seared Scallops are a simple yet sophisticated dish that showcases the natural sweetness and delicate texture of scallops, enhanced by a rich and tangy lemon-butter sauce.

Rack of Lamb with Mint Pesto

Ingredients:

For the Rack of Lamb:

- 2 racks of lamb (about 8 bones each), frenched
- Salt and freshly ground black pepper
- 2 tbsp olive oil
- 2 tbsp Dijon mustard
- 2 tbsp chopped fresh rosemary

For the Mint Pesto:

- 1 cup fresh mint leaves
- 1/2 cup fresh parsley leaves
- 1/4 cup pine nuts or walnuts
- 1/2 cup grated Parmesan cheese
- 1/2 cup olive oil
- 2 garlic cloves
- Juice of 1 lemon
- Salt and freshly ground black pepper, to taste

Instructions:

1. **Prepare the Lamb:**
    - Preheat your oven to 400°F (200°C).
    - Season the racks of lamb generously with salt and pepper. Rub them with olive oil, Dijon mustard, and chopped rosemary.
    - Place the racks of lamb on a rack in a roasting pan, bone side down.
2. **Roast the Lamb:**
    - Roast in the preheated oven for 20-25 minutes for medium-rare, or until the internal temperature reaches 125°F (52°C). Adjust the cooking time if you prefer a different level of doneness.
    - Remove from the oven and let the lamb rest for 10 minutes before slicing.
3. **Make the Mint Pesto:**
    - While the lamb is roasting, combine the mint leaves, parsley, pine nuts (or walnuts), Parmesan cheese, garlic, and lemon juice in a food processor or blender.
    - With the motor running, gradually add the olive oil until the pesto reaches your desired consistency. Season with salt and pepper to taste.
4. **Serve:**
    - Slice the racks of lamb between the bones into individual chops.
    - Spoon the mint pesto over the lamb or serve it on the side as a dipping sauce.

5. **Enjoy:**
    - Serve with your choice of sides, such as roasted potatoes, vegetables, or a fresh salad.

Rack of Lamb with Mint Pesto is a refined and flavorful dish that combines the succulent taste of roasted lamb with the vibrant, fresh flavors of mint pesto, perfect for a special occasion or a gourmet meal.

Lobster Ravioli

Ingredients:

For the Ravioli Filling:

- 1 cup cooked lobster meat, finely chopped
- 1/2 cup ricotta cheese
- 1/4 cup grated Parmesan cheese
- 2 tbsp unsalted butter, melted
- 1 tbsp fresh lemon juice
- 1 tbsp chopped fresh chives or parsley
- Salt and freshly ground black pepper, to taste

For the Ravioli Dough:

- 2 cups all-purpose flour
- 3 large eggs
- 1/4 tsp salt
- 1 tbsp olive oil

For the Sauce:

- 4 tbsp unsalted butter
- 1 cup heavy cream
- 1/4 cup grated Parmesan cheese
- 1 tbsp fresh lemon juice
- Salt and freshly ground black pepper, to taste
- Fresh chives or parsley, chopped (for garnish)

Instructions:

1. **Prepare the Dough:**
   - In a large bowl or on a clean surface, make a mound of flour with a well in the center. Crack the eggs into the well and add the salt and olive oil.
   - Gradually mix the flour into the eggs until a dough forms. Knead the dough on a floured surface for about 8-10 minutes, until smooth and elastic.
   - Wrap the dough in plastic wrap and let it rest for 30 minutes at room temperature.
2. **Prepare the Filling:**
   - In a bowl, combine the chopped lobster meat, ricotta cheese, Parmesan cheese, melted butter, lemon juice, and chives. Season with salt and pepper. Mix well and set aside.
3. **Roll Out the Dough:**
   - Divide the dough into two equal portions. Roll out one portion of the dough on a floured surface or using a pasta machine, until very thin (about 1/16-inch thick).

4. **Form the Ravioli:**
    - Using a spoon or a piping bag, place small dollops of the lobster filling onto the rolled-out dough, spacing them about 1 inch apart.
    - Roll out the second portion of dough and place it over the filled dough. Press around each dollop to seal, making sure there are no air bubbles.
    - Cut the ravioli into squares or circles using a knife or ravioli cutter. Press the edges with a fork to seal completely.
5. **Cook the Ravioli:**
    - Bring a large pot of salted water to a boil. Gently drop the ravioli into the boiling water and cook for 3-4 minutes, or until they float to the surface and are tender. Be careful not to overcrowd the pot.
    - Remove the ravioli with a slotted spoon and set aside.
6. **Prepare the Sauce:**
    - In a large skillet, melt the butter over medium heat. Add the heavy cream and bring to a simmer. Cook for 2-3 minutes until slightly thickened.
    - Stir in the Parmesan cheese and lemon juice. Season with salt and pepper.
7. **Serve:**
    - Toss the cooked ravioli in the sauce to coat or serve the sauce over the ravioli.
    - Garnish with chopped chives or parsley and additional Parmesan cheese if desired.
8. **Enjoy:**
    - Serve immediately for the best texture and flavor.

Lobster Ravioli is a luxurious and flavorful dish that pairs tender, homemade pasta with a rich lobster filling and a creamy sauce, making it perfect for a special occasion or a gourmet dinner.

Lobster Thermidor

Ingredients:

- 2 whole lobsters (about 1 1/2 lbs each)
- 2 tbsp unsalted butter
- 1 small shallot, finely chopped
- 2 garlic cloves, minced
- 1/4 cup dry white wine
- 1/2 cup heavy cream
- 1/2 cup grated Gruyère cheese
- 1/4 cup grated Parmesan cheese
- 1 tbsp Dijon mustard
- 1 tbsp fresh lemon juice
- 1 tbsp fresh tarragon, chopped (or 1 tsp dried tarragon)
- 1/4 tsp paprika
- Salt and freshly ground black pepper, to taste
- 1/4 cup breadcrumbs (for topping)
- Fresh parsley, chopped (for garnish)

Instructions:

1. **Prepare the Lobsters:**
    - Bring a large pot of salted water to a boil. Add the lobsters and cook for 8-10 minutes, or until they are bright red and cooked through.
    - Remove the lobsters from the pot and let them cool. Once cool enough to handle, remove the meat from the shells. Chop the lobster meat into bite-sized pieces and set aside.
    - Reserve the lobster shells for serving.
2. **Make the Sauce:**
    - In a large skillet, melt the butter over medium heat. Add the chopped shallot and cook until softened, about 3-4 minutes.
    - Add the minced garlic and cook for another 1 minute, until fragrant.
    - Deglaze the skillet with the white wine, scraping up any browned bits from the bottom. Cook until the wine has reduced by half.
    - Stir in the heavy cream and bring to a simmer. Cook until the sauce has thickened slightly, about 5 minutes.
    - Remove the skillet from heat and stir in the Gruyère cheese, Parmesan cheese, Dijon mustard, lemon juice, and tarragon. Season with paprika, salt, and pepper. Mix until the cheese is melted and the sauce is smooth.
3. **Combine Lobster and Sauce:**
    - Gently fold the chopped lobster meat into the sauce, ensuring the meat is well coated.
4. **Stuff the Lobster Shells:**

    - Preheat your oven to 375°F (190°C).
    - Spoon the lobster mixture into the reserved lobster shells, packing it in slightly.
5. **Prepare the Topping:**
    - In a small bowl, mix the breadcrumbs with a little melted butter or olive oil.
    - Sprinkle the breadcrumb mixture evenly over the stuffed lobster shells.
6. **Bake:**
    - Place the stuffed lobster shells on a baking sheet and bake in the preheated oven for 10-12 minutes, or until the topping is golden brown and the filling is heated through.
7. **Serve:**
    - Garnish with freshly chopped parsley and serve immediately.

Lobster Thermidor is a rich and elegant dish featuring tender lobster meat in a creamy, cheesy sauce, baked to perfection. It's perfect for special occasions or a luxurious dinner.

Beef Bourguignon

Ingredients:

- 2 lbs beef chuck, cut into 1-inch cubes
- Salt and freshly ground black pepper
- 1/4 cup all-purpose flour
- 2 tbsp olive oil
- 4 slices bacon, diced
- 1 large onion, chopped
- 2 carrots, peeled and sliced
- 2 garlic cloves, minced
- 1 cup dry red wine (such as Burgundy or Cabernet Sauvignon)
- 2 cups beef broth
- 1 tbsp tomato paste
- 1 tbsp fresh thyme leaves (or 1 tsp dried thyme)
- 2 bay leaves
- 1 cup pearl onions, peeled
- 1 cup mushrooms, quartered
- 2 tbsp unsalted butter
- Fresh parsley, chopped (for garnish)

Instructions:

1. **Prepare the Beef:**
   - Season the beef cubes with salt and pepper, then coat lightly with flour, shaking off excess.
2. **Brown the Beef:**
   - Heat olive oil in a large Dutch oven or heavy pot over medium-high heat. Brown the beef in batches, ensuring it's well-seared on all sides. Remove the beef and set aside.
3. **Cook the Bacon:**
   - In the same pot, add the diced bacon and cook until crispy. Remove the bacon with a slotted spoon and set aside.
4. **Sauté Vegetables:**
   - Add the chopped onion and carrots to the pot. Cook until softened, about 5 minutes. Stir in the garlic and cook for another minute.
5. **Deglaze and Simmer:**
   - Return the beef and bacon to the pot. Stir in the tomato paste and cook for 1 minute.
   - Pour in the red wine, scraping up any browned bits from the bottom of the pot. Bring to a simmer and cook for 5 minutes.
6. **Add Broth and Herbs:**

- Add the beef broth, thyme, and bay leaves. Bring to a simmer, then cover and transfer to the preheated oven.

7. **Bake:**
    - Bake in the oven for 2.5 to 3 hours, or until the beef is tender and the sauce is thickened.
8. **Prepare the Vegetables:**
    - While the beef is baking, melt butter in a skillet over medium heat. Add the pearl onions and cook until browned and tender. Add the mushrooms and cook until browned.
9. **Combine and Serve:**
    - Stir the sautéed onions and mushrooms into the beef stew after it has finished baking. Remove the bay leaves.
    - Garnish with fresh parsley and serve hot with crusty bread, mashed potatoes, or noodles.

Beef Bourguignon is a rich, comforting stew with tender beef, aromatic vegetables, and a deep, savory sauce, perfect for a hearty meal or special occasion.

Chilean Sea Bass

Ingredients:

- 4 (6 oz each) Chilean sea bass fillets
- Salt and freshly ground black pepper
- 2 tbsp olive oil
- 1 lemon, thinly sliced
- 2 cloves garlic, minced
- 1/4 cup white wine or vegetable broth
- 2 tbsp fresh parsley, chopped
- 1 tbsp fresh dill or thyme, chopped (optional)

Instructions:

1. **Preheat the Oven:**
   - Preheat your oven to 400°F (200°C).
2. **Prepare the Fillets:**
   - Pat the sea bass fillets dry with paper towels. Season both sides with salt and pepper.
3. **Sear the Sea Bass:**
   - Heat olive oil in a large ovenproof skillet over medium-high heat. Add the sea bass fillets, skin side down, and sear for 3-4 minutes until the skin is crispy and golden brown.
4. **Add Flavorings:**
   - Flip the fillets and add minced garlic to the skillet. Sauté briefly until fragrant, about 30 seconds.
5. **Deglaze and Bake:**
   - Pour in the white wine or vegetable broth. Arrange lemon slices over the fillets.
   - Transfer the skillet to the preheated oven and bake for 8-10 minutes, or until the fish is opaque and flakes easily with a fork.
6. **Garnish and Serve:**
   - Remove from the oven and sprinkle with chopped parsley and optional dill or thyme.
   - Serve immediately with your choice of sides, such as roasted vegetables, rice, or a fresh salad.

Chilean Sea Bass is known for its rich, buttery flavor and tender texture, making it a luxurious choice for a simple yet elegant meal.

Chateaubriand Steak

Ingredients:

- 1 center-cut beef tenderloin (about 1.5-2 lbs), trimmed
- Salt and freshly ground black pepper
- 2 tbsp olive oil
- 2 tbsp unsalted butter
- 2 cloves garlic, minced
- 2 sprigs fresh rosemary or thyme (optional)
- 1 cup red wine (such as Cabernet Sauvignon)
- 1 cup beef broth
- 1 tbsp Dijon mustard
- 1 tbsp fresh parsley, chopped (for garnish)

Instructions:

1. **Prepare the Steak:**
   - Preheat your oven to 400°F (200°C).
   - Season the beef tenderloin generously with salt and pepper.
2. **Sear the Steak:**
   - Heat olive oil in a large ovenproof skillet over medium-high heat. Add the tenderloin and sear on all sides until browned, about 3-4 minutes per side.
3. **Add Flavorings:**
   - Add the butter, garlic, and optional rosemary or thyme to the skillet. Baste the steak with the melted butter and aromatics for an additional 2 minutes.
4. **Roast:**
   - Transfer the skillet to the preheated oven and roast for 15-20 minutes, or until the internal temperature reaches 130°F (54°C) for medium-rare, or to your desired doneness.
5. **Rest the Steak:**
   - Remove the skillet from the oven and let the steak rest for 10 minutes before slicing.
6. **Prepare the Sauce:**
   - While the steak is resting, place the skillet over medium heat on the stovetop. Add red wine and scrape up any browned bits from the bottom of the pan.
   - Stir in the beef broth and Dijon mustard. Simmer until the sauce is reduced and slightly thickened, about 5-7 minutes. Adjust seasoning with salt and pepper if needed.
7. **Serve:**
   - Slice the Chateaubriand into thick steaks and serve with the red wine sauce drizzled over the top.
   - Garnish with fresh parsley.

Chateaubriand Steak is a luxurious cut of beef, ideal for special occasions, featuring a tender texture and rich flavor complemented by a simple yet elegant red wine sauce.

Coq au Vin

Ingredients:

- 4-6 chicken thighs and drumsticks, skin-on and bone-in
- Salt and freshly ground black pepper
- 2 tbsp olive oil
- 4 slices bacon, diced
- 1 large onion, chopped
- 2 carrots, peeled and sliced
- 2 garlic cloves, minced
- 2 tbsp tomato paste
- 2 cups red wine (such as Burgundy or Pinot Noir)
- 1 cup chicken broth
- 1 tbsp fresh thyme leaves (or 1 tsp dried thyme)
- 2 bay leaves
- 1 cup mushrooms, quartered
- 1 cup pearl onions, peeled
- 2 tbsp unsalted butter
- Fresh parsley, chopped (for garnish)

Instructions:

1. **Prepare the Chicken:**
   - Season the chicken pieces with salt and pepper.
2. **Brown the Chicken:**
   - Heat olive oil in a large Dutch oven or heavy pot over medium-high heat. Brown the chicken pieces on all sides, working in batches if necessary. Remove and set aside.
3. **Cook the Bacon and Vegetables:**
   - In the same pot, add the diced bacon and cook until crispy. Remove the bacon with a slotted spoon and set aside.
   - Add the chopped onion and carrots to the pot. Cook until softened, about 5 minutes. Stir in the minced garlic and cook for an additional minute.
   - Add the tomato paste and cook for 2 minutes, stirring frequently.
4. **Deglaze and Simmer:**
   - Pour in the red wine and chicken broth, scraping up any browned bits from the bottom of the pot. Bring to a simmer.
   - Return the chicken and bacon to the pot. Add the thyme and bay leaves. Ensure the chicken is mostly submerged in the liquid.
5. **Cook:**
   - Cover the pot and transfer to the preheated oven. Bake for 45-60 minutes, or until the chicken is tender and cooked through.
6. **Prepare the Mushrooms and Pearl Onions:**

- While the chicken is cooking, melt butter in a skillet over medium heat. Add the mushrooms and cook until browned and tender. Add the pearl onions and cook until browned and tender, about 5-7 minutes.
7. **Combine and Serve:**
    - Stir the mushrooms and pearl onions into the chicken stew during the last 15 minutes of cooking.
    - Remove the bay leaves before serving.
8. **Garnish and Enjoy:**
    - Garnish with chopped fresh parsley and serve with crusty bread, mashed potatoes, or rice.

Coq au Vin is a classic French dish that features chicken slow-cooked in red wine with bacon, vegetables, and aromatic herbs, resulting in a rich, flavorful stew perfect for a comforting meal.

Peking Duck

Ingredients:

For the Duck:

- 1 whole duck (about 5-6 lbs), cleaned and patted dry
- 1 tbsp salt
- 1 tbsp sugar
- 2 tbsp soy sauce
- 2 tbsp rice vinegar
- 2 tbsp honey
- 2 tbsp hoisin sauce
- 1 cup water

For the Glaze:

- 1/4 cup honey
- 2 tbsp soy sauce
- 1 tbsp rice vinegar

For Serving:

- Mandarin pancakes or thin Chinese pancakes
- Hoisin sauce
- Sliced scallions
- Cucumber, thinly sliced

Instructions:

1. **Prepare the Duck:**
    - Preheat your oven to 375°F (190°C).
    - Remove any remaining feathers from the duck and trim excess fat. Pat the duck dry with paper towels.
2. **Season and Marinate:**
    - Rub the duck inside and out with salt and sugar. Let it sit at room temperature for 30 minutes.
    - Mix soy sauce, rice vinegar, honey, and hoisin sauce in a bowl. Brush this mixture all over the duck.
3. **Dry the Duck:**
    - To achieve crispy skin, it's crucial to dry the duck thoroughly. Hang the duck in a cool, dry place (or in the refrigerator) for 4-6 hours, uncovered. Alternatively, use a fan to help dry the skin.
4. **Roast the Duck:**

- Place the duck on a rack in a roasting pan, breast side up. Roast in the preheated oven for 1.5-2 hours, or until the skin is golden brown and crispy. Baste occasionally with the drippings.
5. **Prepare the Glaze:**
    - While the duck is roasting, combine honey, soy sauce, and rice vinegar in a small saucepan. Heat over medium heat until the mixture is well combined and slightly thickened. Set aside.
6. **Finish the Duck:**
    - About 20 minutes before the duck is done, brush the glaze all over the duck. Continue roasting until the skin is crispy and caramelized.
7. **Rest and Carve:**
    - Remove the duck from the oven and let it rest for 10 minutes. Carve the duck into thin slices, focusing on the skin and meat.
8. **Serve:**
    - Serve the duck with Mandarin pancakes, hoisin sauce, sliced scallions, and cucumber. Place a few slices of duck onto a pancake, spread with hoisin sauce, and top with scallions and cucumber.

Tips:

- If you don't have Mandarin pancakes, you can use flour tortillas or make your own pancakes.
- For extra crispy skin, you can also use a bamboo or metal skewer to hold the duck while roasting, or place it on a rack over the pan to let the fat drain off.

Peking Duck is a renowned Chinese dish celebrated for its crispy skin and succulent meat, served with traditional accompaniments for a delicious and authentic experience.

Duck Confit

Ingredients:

- 4 duck legs (with thighs)
- 1 tbsp salt
- 1 tsp black pepper
- 4 garlic cloves, minced
- 2 sprigs fresh thyme (or 1 tsp dried thyme)
- 1 bay leaf
- 2 cups duck fat (or substitute with vegetable oil)

Instructions:

1. **Prepare the Duck:**
   - Pat the duck legs dry with paper towels. Rub them all over with salt, pepper, minced garlic, thyme, and bay leaf.
2. **Marinate:**
   - Place the duck legs in a covered container and refrigerate for at least 24 hours, preferably 2-3 days. This allows the flavors to penetrate the meat.
3. **Preheat Oven:**
   - Preheat your oven to 275°F (135°C).
4. **Cook the Duck:**
   - Rinse the duck legs under cold water to remove excess salt and spices. Pat them dry again.
   - Place the duck legs in a large ovenproof pot or Dutch oven. Cover the legs with duck fat (or oil). If necessary, add more fat to ensure the legs are fully submerged.
5. **Slow-Cook:**
   - Place the pot in the preheated oven. Cook the duck slowly for 2.5 to 3 hours, or until the meat is tender and easily pulls away from the bone.
6. **Crisp the Skin:**
   - Once cooked, remove the duck legs from the fat and let them drain on a paper towel.
   - For crispy skin, heat a skillet over medium-high heat. Add the duck legs skin-side down and cook until the skin is crispy and browned, about 5-7 minutes.
7. **Serve:**
   - Duck confit can be served as is or used in other dishes like salads, tacos, or pasta. Serve with roasted vegetables, potatoes, or a side salad.
8. **Storage:**
   - If storing, keep the duck legs submerged in the fat in an airtight container in the refrigerator for up to 2 weeks. The fat helps preserve the duck.

Duck Confit is a traditional French dish that features slow-cooked duck legs in rich duck fat, resulting in incredibly tender meat and a perfectly crispy skin.

Bouillabaisse

Ingredients:

For the Broth:

- 2 tbsp olive oil
- 1 large onion, chopped
- 2 leeks, white parts only, cleaned and sliced
- 2 celery stalks, chopped
- 4 garlic cloves, minced
- 1 cup white wine
- 1 can (14.5 oz) crushed tomatoes
- 4 cups fish stock or water
- 1 tsp saffron threads
- 1 tsp dried thyme
- 1 bay leaf
- Salt and freshly ground black pepper, to taste

For the Seafood:

- 1 lb firm white fish (such as cod, haddock, or snapper), cut into chunks
- 1/2 lb mussels, cleaned and debearded
- 1/2 lb clams, cleaned
- 1/2 lb shrimp, peeled and deveined
- 1/2 lb squid, cleaned and sliced into rings

For Serving:

- Rouille sauce (recipe below)
- Crusty baguette or toast

For Rouille Sauce:

- 1/2 cup mayonnaise
- 2 garlic cloves, minced
- 1/2 tsp saffron threads
- 1/2 tsp paprika
- 1 tbsp lemon juice
- Salt, to taste

Instructions:

1. **Prepare the Broth:**
   - Heat olive oil in a large pot or Dutch oven over medium heat. Add the onion, leeks, celery, and garlic. Sauté until softened, about 5 minutes.
   - Pour in the white wine and cook until reduced by half.

- Stir in the crushed tomatoes, fish stock (or water), saffron, thyme, bay leaf, salt, and pepper. Bring to a simmer and cook for 20 minutes to allow the flavors to meld.
2. **Cook the Seafood:**
    - Add the fish chunks to the simmering broth and cook for 5 minutes.
    - Add the mussels and clams. Cover and cook for another 5-7 minutes, or until the mussels and clams have opened.
    - Stir in the shrimp and squid. Cook for an additional 3-4 minutes, or until the shrimp are pink and opaque and the squid is tender.
3. **Prepare the Rouille Sauce:**
    - In a bowl, mix together the mayonnaise, garlic, saffron, paprika, lemon juice, and salt. Adjust seasoning to taste.
4. **Serve:**
    - Ladle the Bouillabaisse into bowls, ensuring each serving includes a variety of seafood.
    - Serve with crusty baguette or toast, and a dollop of rouille sauce on the side or spread on the bread.
5. **Garnish (Optional):**
    - Garnish with chopped fresh parsley for added color and flavor.

Bouillabaisse is a traditional Provençal seafood stew, known for its rich, aromatic broth and a variety of fresh seafood. The rouille sauce adds a spicy, garlicky kick that complements the dish beautifully.

Veal Osso Buco

Ingredients:

For the Osso Buco:

- 4 veal shanks (about 1.5-2 inches thick)
- Salt and freshly ground black pepper
- 1/4 cup all-purpose flour
- 2 tbsp olive oil
- 2 tbsp unsalted butter
- 1 large onion, chopped
- 2 carrots, peeled and chopped
- 2 celery stalks, chopped
- 4 garlic cloves, minced
- 1 cup dry white wine
- 1 cup chicken broth
- 1 can (14.5 oz) crushed tomatoes
- 2 tsp fresh thyme leaves (or 1 tsp dried thyme)
- 2 bay leaves

For the Gremolata:

- 1/4 cup fresh parsley, chopped
- 2 garlic cloves, minced
- Zest of 1 lemon

Instructions:

1. **Prepare the Veal:**
   - Preheat your oven to 325°F (165°C).
   - Season the veal shanks with salt and pepper, then lightly coat them with flour, shaking off any excess.
2. **Sear the Shanks:**
   - Heat olive oil and butter in a large Dutch oven or heavy pot over medium-high heat. Add the veal shanks and brown them on all sides, about 3-4 minutes per side. Remove the shanks and set aside.
3. **Cook the Vegetables:**
   - In the same pot, add the chopped onion, carrots, and celery. Sauté until softened, about 5-7 minutes. Stir in the minced garlic and cook for an additional minute.
4. **Deglaze and Simmer:**
   - Pour in the white wine and scrape up any browned bits from the bottom of the pot. Cook until the wine has reduced by half.

        - Stir in the chicken broth, crushed tomatoes, thyme, and bay leaves. Bring to a simmer.
5. **Braise the Veal:**
        - Return the veal shanks to the pot, ensuring they are mostly submerged in the liquid.
        - Cover the pot and transfer it to the preheated oven. Braise for 2.5 to 3 hours, or until the veal is tender and the meat is falling off the bone.
6. **Prepare the Gremolata:**
        - While the veal is cooking, mix together the parsley, minced garlic, and lemon zest in a small bowl. Set aside.
7. **Serve:**
        - Remove the veal shanks from the pot and discard the bay leaves.
        - Spoon the sauce and vegetables over the veal shanks.
        - Garnish with gremolata just before serving.

Veal Osso Buco is a classic Italian dish featuring slow-cooked veal shanks in a rich tomato and wine sauce, complemented by a fresh gremolata for added brightness and flavor. It pairs beautifully with risotto, polenta, or mashed potatoes.

Salmon en Papillote

Ingredients:

- 4 (6 oz each) salmon fillets
- Salt and freshly ground black pepper
- 1 lemon, thinly sliced
- 4 sprigs fresh thyme or dill (or 1 tsp dried)
- 1 cup cherry tomatoes, halved
- 1 cup thinly sliced zucchini
- 1 cup thinly sliced bell peppers (red, yellow, or orange)
- 2 cloves garlic, minced
- 2 tbsp olive oil
- 1/4 cup white wine or vegetable broth (optional)
- 4 sheets parchment paper (about 12x16 inches each)

Instructions:

1. **Preheat the Oven:**
   - Preheat your oven to 400°F (200°C).
2. **Prepare the Vegetables:**
   - In a bowl, toss the cherry tomatoes, zucchini, bell peppers, and minced garlic with olive oil, salt, and pepper.
3. **Prepare the Parchment Paper:**
   - Fold each parchment sheet in half, then unfold. Place each piece on a baking sheet.
4. **Assemble the Packets:**
   - Place a portion of the vegetable mixture in the center of each parchment sheet.
   - Season the salmon fillets with salt and pepper, then place one fillet on top of the vegetables.
   - Top each salmon fillet with a few lemon slices and a sprig of thyme or dill.
   - If using, pour a small splash of white wine or vegetable broth over each fillet.
5. **Seal the Packets:**
   - Fold the parchment paper over the salmon and vegetables, creating a tight seal by folding and crimping the edges. Make sure the packets are sealed well to trap the steam.
6. **Bake:**
   - Place the parchment packets on a baking sheet and bake in the preheated oven for 15-20 minutes, or until the salmon is opaque and flakes easily with a fork.
7. **Serve:**
   - Carefully open the packets (beware of hot steam) and transfer the salmon and vegetables to serving plates.
   - Serve immediately with a side of rice, quinoa, or a simple green salad.

Tips:

- You can customize the vegetables based on your preference or seasonal availability.
- For added flavor, consider adding a splash of lemon juice or a sprinkle of fresh herbs before sealing the packets.

Salmon en Papillote is a healthy, flavorful dish that's easy to prepare, and the parchment paper method ensures the fish remains moist and tender while infusing it with aromatic flavors.

Filet Mignon

Ingredients:

- 4 (6 oz each) filet mignon steaks, about 1.5 inches thick
- Salt and freshly ground black pepper
- 2 tbsp olive oil
- 2 tbsp unsalted butter
- 2 cloves garlic, minced
- 2 sprigs fresh thyme or rosemary (optional)
- 1 cup red wine (optional, for sauce)
- 1/2 cup beef broth (optional, for sauce)
- 1 tbsp Dijon mustard (optional, for sauce)
- 1 tbsp fresh parsley, chopped (for garnish)

Instructions:

1. **Prepare the Steaks:**
    - Remove the filet mignon steaks from the refrigerator about 30 minutes before cooking to bring them to room temperature. Season both sides generously with salt and pepper.
2. **Sear the Steaks:**
    - Heat olive oil in a large skillet or cast-iron pan over high heat until shimmering.
    - Add the steaks and sear for 3-4 minutes on each side, or until a deep brown crust forms. For medium-rare, aim for an internal temperature of 130°F (54°C). Adjust cooking time to achieve your desired doneness.
3. **Add Butter and Aromatics:**
    - Lower the heat to medium. Add butter, minced garlic, and optional thyme or rosemary to the pan. Baste the steaks with the melted butter and aromatics for added flavor.
4. **Rest the Steaks:**
    - Remove the steaks from the pan and let them rest on a plate covered with foil for 5-10 minutes. This allows the juices to redistribute.
5. **Prepare the Optional Sauce:**
    - While the steaks are resting, deglaze the pan with red wine, scraping up any browned bits from the bottom. Cook for 2-3 minutes until reduced by half.
    - Stir in beef broth and Dijon mustard, simmering for an additional 3-4 minutes until the sauce thickens slightly. Adjust seasoning with salt and pepper if needed.
6. **Serve:**
    - Slice the filet mignon if desired and serve with the optional sauce drizzled over the top.
    - Garnish with chopped parsley.

Tips:

- For a more precise doneness, use a meat thermometer.
- Letting the steak rest after cooking ensures a juicier and more flavorful result.

Filet Mignon is renowned for its exceptional tenderness and rich taste, making it a popular choice for special occasions and fine dining experiences.

Beef Tenderloin with Red Wine Sauce

Ingredients:

For the Beef Tenderloin:

- 1 (2-3 lbs) whole beef tenderloin, trimmed
- Salt and freshly ground black pepper
- 2 tbsp olive oil
- 2 tbsp unsalted butter
- 2 cloves garlic, minced
- 2 sprigs fresh thyme or rosemary (optional)

For the Red Wine Sauce:

- 1 cup red wine (such as Cabernet Sauvignon or Merlot)
- 1 cup beef broth
- 1 small shallot, finely chopped
- 2 cloves garlic, minced
- 2 tbsp unsalted butter
- 1 tbsp all-purpose flour
- 1 tsp fresh thyme leaves (or 1/2 tsp dried thyme)
- 1 tsp Dijon mustard
- Salt and freshly ground black pepper, to taste

Instructions:

1. **Prepare the Beef Tenderloin:**
    - Preheat your oven to 400°F (200°C).
    - Season the beef tenderloin generously with salt and pepper.
    - Heat olive oil in a large ovenproof skillet over medium-high heat. Sear the tenderloin on all sides until browned, about 2-3 minutes per side.
    - Add the butter and minced garlic to the skillet, basting the tenderloin with the melted butter. Add optional thyme or rosemary for additional flavor.
    - Transfer the skillet to the preheated oven and roast for 20-25 minutes, or until the internal temperature reaches 130°F (54°C) for medium-rare. Adjust time for desired doneness.
    - Remove the tenderloin from the oven and let it rest for 10 minutes before slicing.
2. **Prepare the Red Wine Sauce:**
    - While the tenderloin is roasting, make the sauce. In a saucepan, melt 2 tbsp butter over medium heat. Add the shallot and garlic, and sauté until softened, about 2-3 minutes.
    - Stir in the flour and cook for 1 minute to create a roux.

- - Gradually whisk in the red wine and beef broth. Add thyme and Dijon mustard. Bring to a simmer and cook until the sauce is reduced by half and slightly thickened, about 10-15 minutes.
  - Season with salt and pepper to taste. Strain the sauce through a fine-mesh sieve if you prefer a smoother texture.
3. **Serve:**
    - Slice the rested beef tenderloin into medallions and arrange on serving plates.
    - Spoon the red wine sauce over the sliced beef.
    - Garnish with additional fresh thyme or rosemary if desired.

Tips:

- For a precise doneness, use a meat thermometer.
- Letting the beef rest is crucial for a juicy result.

Beef Tenderloin with Red Wine Sauce is a refined and flavorful dish that combines the tenderness of the beef with a rich, aromatic sauce, making it a standout choice for any special meal.

Moroccan Tagine

Ingredients:

For the Tagine:

- 2 lbs lamb or chicken, cut into chunks (or use beef)
- 2 tbsp olive oil
- 1 large onion, chopped
- 3 garlic cloves, minced
- 2 tsp ground cumin
- 2 tsp ground coriander
- 1 tsp ground cinnamon
- 1/2 tsp ground turmeric
- 1/2 tsp paprika
- 1/4 tsp ground ginger
- 1/4 tsp cayenne pepper (optional, for heat)
- 1 can (14.5 oz) diced tomatoes
- 1 cup chicken or beef broth
- 1 cup dried apricots or dates, chopped
- 1/2 cup almonds, toasted (optional)
- 1 cup green olives, pitted and sliced
- 1 tbsp honey or brown sugar (optional, for sweetness)
- Salt and freshly ground black pepper, to taste

For Serving:

- Cooked couscous or rice
- Fresh cilantro or parsley, chopped

Instructions:

1. **Prepare the Meat:**
    - Season the meat with salt and pepper. Heat olive oil in a large tagine pot or Dutch oven over medium-high heat. Brown the meat on all sides, then remove and set aside.
2. **Cook the Aromatics:**
    - In the same pot, add the chopped onion and cook until softened, about 5 minutes. Add the garlic and cook for another minute.
3. **Add Spices:**
    - Stir in the cumin, coriander, cinnamon, turmeric, paprika, ginger, and cayenne pepper. Cook for 1-2 minutes until the spices are fragrant.
4. **Simmer the Tagine:**

- - Return the browned meat to the pot. Add diced tomatoes and broth. Bring to a simmer.
  - Stir in the dried apricots or dates and honey (if using). Cover and reduce heat to low. Simmer gently for 1.5 to 2 hours, or until the meat is tender and the sauce is thickened.
5. **Finish and Garnish:**
    - Add the sliced olives and toasted almonds (if using) in the last 15 minutes of cooking. Adjust seasoning with salt and pepper as needed.
6. **Serve:**
    - Serve the tagine over cooked couscous or rice. Garnish with chopped fresh cilantro or parsley.

Tips:

- Traditional tagines often include preserved lemons and additional spices like saffron, which you can add for extra flavor.
- If using chicken, adjust the cooking time to about 45 minutes to 1 hour.

Moroccan Tagine is a fragrant and hearty stew that combines savory spices with sweet and tangy elements, creating a deeply satisfying dish perfect for sharing with family and friends.

Braised Short Ribs

Ingredients:

- 4 lbs beef short ribs, bone-in
- Salt and freshly ground black pepper
- 2 tbsp vegetable oil
- 1 large onion, chopped
- 2 carrots, peeled and chopped
- 2 celery stalks, chopped
- 4 garlic cloves, minced
- 2 tbsp tomato paste
- 1 cup red wine (such as Cabernet Sauvignon)
- 2 cups beef broth
- 1 cup canned diced tomatoes (with juices)
- 2 sprigs fresh thyme or 1 tsp dried thyme
- 2 bay leaves
- 2 tbsp soy sauce (optional, for extra depth)
- 2 tbsp all-purpose flour (optional, for thickening)

Instructions:

1. **Prepare the Ribs:**
   - Preheat your oven to 325°F (165°C).
   - Season the short ribs generously with salt and pepper.
2. **Sear the Ribs:**
   - Heat vegetable oil in a large Dutch oven or ovenproof pot over medium-high heat. Add the short ribs and sear on all sides until browned, about 3-4 minutes per side. Remove the ribs and set aside.
3. **Cook the Vegetables:**
   - In the same pot, add onion, carrots, and celery. Cook until softened, about 5-7 minutes. Stir in garlic and cook for another minute.
   - Add tomato paste and cook for 2 minutes, stirring frequently.
4. **Deglaze and Simmer:**
   - Pour in the red wine and scrape up any browned bits from the bottom of the pot. Simmer until the wine is reduced by half, about 5 minutes.
   - Stir in beef broth, diced tomatoes, thyme, bay leaves, and soy sauce (if using). Bring to a simmer.
5. **Braise the Ribs:**
   - Return the short ribs to the pot, making sure they are mostly submerged in the liquid.
   - Cover the pot and transfer it to the preheated oven. Braise for 2.5 to 3 hours, or until the meat is tender and easily falls off the bone.
6. **Finish the Sauce:**

- Remove the short ribs from the pot and let them rest.
- If you prefer a thicker sauce, combine 2 tbsp flour with 2 tbsp butter to make a paste. Stir the paste into the simmering sauce and cook until thickened, about 5 minutes. Adjust seasoning with salt and pepper.

7. **Serve:**
   - Serve the braised short ribs with the sauce spooned over the top. Pair with mashed potatoes, polenta, or a hearty vegetable side.

Tips:

- For best results, braise the short ribs a day ahead and let them rest in the refrigerator overnight. This allows the flavors to develop and the fat to solidify, making it easier to remove.

Braised Short Ribs are a comforting and indulgent dish, perfect for special occasions or cozy dinners. The slow cooking process results in fall-apart tender meat and a deeply flavorful sauce.

Lobster Newberg

Ingredients:

- 1 lb lobster meat (cooked and chopped into bite-sized pieces)
- 2 tbsp unsalted butter
- 1 small onion, finely chopped
- 1 cup mushrooms, sliced
- 1/2 cup dry white wine
- 1 cup heavy cream
- 1/4 cup milk
- 3 large egg yolks
- 1/4 cup sherry or brandy
- 1/4 tsp ground nutmeg
- 1/4 tsp paprika
- Salt and freshly ground black pepper, to taste
- 2 tbsp chopped fresh parsley (for garnish)
- 4 slices of toast or puff pastry shells (optional, for serving)

Instructions:

1. **Prepare the Lobster:**
   - If not using pre-cooked lobster, boil live lobsters in salted water for about 8-10 minutes. Remove the meat from the shells and chop into bite-sized pieces. Set aside.
2. **Cook the Vegetables:**
   - Melt butter in a large skillet over medium heat. Add the chopped onion and mushrooms, and cook until softened, about 5 minutes.
3. **Deglaze and Simmer:**
   - Add white wine to the skillet and cook until reduced by half. Stir in the heavy cream and milk, and bring to a gentle simmer.
4. **Prepare the Egg Mixture:**
   - In a small bowl, whisk together the egg yolks. Slowly add a small amount of the hot cream mixture to the egg yolks, whisking constantly to temper them. This prevents the eggs from curdling.
5. **Combine Ingredients:**
   - Slowly pour the egg yolk mixture back into the skillet, stirring constantly. Cook gently until the sauce thickens, about 3-5 minutes. Be careful not to overheat or boil, as this can cause the sauce to curdle.
6. **Add Lobster and Season:**
   - Stir in the chopped lobster meat. Add sherry or brandy, nutmeg, paprika, salt, and pepper. Cook for an additional 2-3 minutes until the lobster is heated through and the flavors are combined.
7. **Serve:**

- Spoon the Lobster Newberg mixture onto slices of toast or into puff pastry shells, if using. Garnish with chopped fresh parsley.

Tips:

- For an extra touch of elegance, you can also serve Lobster Newberg over a bed of rice or in individual ramekins for a more formal presentation.
- Ensure the sauce does not boil after adding the egg yolks to prevent curdling.

Lobster Newberg is a rich and indulgent dish, known for its creamy texture and sophisticated flavors, making it a perfect choice for an elegant meal or a special celebration.

Roasted Bone Marrow

Ingredients:

- 4 beef marrow bones (cut into 3-4 inch pieces)
- Salt and freshly ground black pepper
- 2 tbsp olive oil
- 2-3 garlic cloves, minced
- 1 tbsp fresh thyme or rosemary, chopped
- 1 lemon, cut into wedges
- Fresh parsley, chopped (for garnish)
- Toasted baguette slices (for serving)

Instructions:

1. **Prepare the Bones:**
   - Preheat your oven to 450°F (230°C).
   - Arrange the marrow bones cut side up on a baking sheet lined with parchment paper or foil.
2. **Season the Bones:**
   - Brush the marrow bones with olive oil and season generously with salt and pepper. Sprinkle minced garlic and chopped thyme or rosemary over the bones.
3. **Roast the Bones:**
   - Roast in the preheated oven for 15-20 minutes, or until the marrow is soft, bubbling, and beginning to brown. The marrow should be creamy and slightly caramelized.
4. **Serve:**
   - Remove from the oven and let the bones cool slightly. Garnish with fresh parsley.
   - Serve with lemon wedges and toasted baguette slices. Scoop the marrow onto the bread and squeeze lemon juice over it for added flavor.

Tips:

- Avoid overcooking the marrow; it should be warm and creamy.
- You can also add a sprinkle of sea salt or additional herbs for extra flavor before serving.

Roasted Bone Marrow is a luxurious treat with a rich, buttery texture, perfect as an appetizer or indulgent snack.

Roasted Bone Marrow

Ingredients:

- 4 beef marrow bones (3-4 inches long, from your butcher)
- Salt and freshly ground black pepper
- 2 tbsp olive oil
- 2-3 garlic cloves, minced
- 1 tbsp fresh rosemary or thyme, chopped (or a mix of both)
- 1 lemon, cut into wedges
- Fresh parsley, chopped (for garnish)
- Toasted baguette slices (for serving)

Instructions:

1. **Prepare the Bones:**
    - Preheat your oven to 450°F (230°C).
    - Arrange the marrow bones cut side up on a baking sheet lined with parchment paper or aluminum foil. If the bones are not pre-cut, ask your butcher to cut them into 3-4 inch sections.
2. **Season the Bones:**
    - Brush the marrow bones lightly with olive oil. Season generously with salt and freshly ground black pepper. Sprinkle the minced garlic and chopped rosemary or thyme evenly over the bones.
3. **Roast the Bones:**
    - Roast in the preheated oven for 15-20 minutes, or until the marrow is soft and beginning to bubble. The marrow should be warm and creamy, with a slightly caramelized top. Be careful not to overcook as it can become greasy and lose its creamy texture.
4. **Serve:**
    - Remove the bones from the oven and let them cool for a few minutes. Garnish with chopped fresh parsley.
    - Serve the roasted marrow with lemon wedges and toasted baguette slices. To eat, scoop the marrow onto the toast and squeeze a bit of lemon juice over it for a bright, fresh flavor.

Tips:

- **Prepping the Bones:** If you have any concerns about the marrow bones being too fatty, you can soak them in cold salted water for a few hours before roasting. This helps to draw out some of the blood and impurities.
- **Serving Suggestions:** For a more elaborate presentation, you can also serve roasted marrow with a side of pickled vegetables or a simple salad.

Roasted Bone Marrow is a decadent treat with a rich, buttery texture that's perfect for special occasions or as a luxurious appetizer.

Foie Gras Burger

Ingredients:

For the Foie Gras:

- 4 slices foie gras (about 1/2 inch thick)
- Salt and freshly ground black pepper
- 2 tbsp all-purpose flour (for dusting)

For the Burger:

- 4 beef burger patties (about 6 oz each)
- Salt and freshly ground black pepper
- 4 burger buns, toasted
- 4 tbsp mayonnaise
- 4 tbsp Dijon mustard
- 1 large shallot, thinly sliced
- 4 slices of cheese (optional, such as Gruyère or Swiss)
- 1 cup arugula or baby spinach
- 4 tbsp fig jam or caramelized onions (optional, for sweetness)

Instructions:

1. **Prepare the Foie Gras:**
    - Season foie gras slices with salt and pepper. Dust lightly with flour.
    - Heat a non-stick skillet over medium-high heat. Sear foie gras for about 30 seconds to 1 minute per side, until golden brown. Remove and set aside on paper towels to drain.
2. **Cook the Beef Patties:**
    - Season beef patties with salt and pepper.
    - Grill or pan-cook patties over medium-high heat until desired doneness is reached (about 4-5 minutes per side for medium-rare). If using cheese, add a slice to each patty during the last minute of cooking and cover to melt.
3. **Prepare the Buns and Condiments:**
    - Toast the burger buns until golden.
    - Spread mayonnaise and Dijon mustard on the bottom half of each bun. Optionally, spread fig jam or caramelized onions on the top half.
4. **Assemble the Burger:**
    - Place the cooked beef patty on the bottom half of each bun.
    - Top with a slice of seared foie gras.
    - Add a few slices of shallot and a handful of arugula or baby spinach.
5. **Finish and Serve:**
    - Close with the top half of the bun. Serve immediately.

Tips:

- **Foie Gras Cooking:** Ensure the foie gras is not overcooked; it should remain rich and creamy.
- **Burger Assembly:** For an extra touch of luxury, consider adding a small amount of truffle oil or a drizzle of balsamic reduction.

The Foie Gras Burger offers an exquisite blend of rich foie gras and a hearty beef patty, elevated with gourmet toppings for a truly indulgent meal.

Wild Mushroom Risotto

Ingredients:

- 1 1/2 cups Arborio rice
- 1 lb wild mushrooms (such as porcini, shiitake, or a mix), cleaned and sliced
- 1 small onion, finely chopped
- 3 garlic cloves, minced
- 1/2 cup dry white wine
- 4 cups chicken or vegetable broth
- 2 tbsp olive oil
- 2 tbsp unsalted butter
- 1/2 cup grated Parmesan cheese
- 2 tbsp fresh parsley, chopped
- Salt and freshly ground black pepper, to taste

Instructions:

1. **Prepare the Broth:**
    - In a saucepan, keep the chicken or vegetable broth warm over low heat.
2. **Cook the Mushrooms:**
    - In a large skillet, heat 1 tbsp of olive oil over medium heat. Add the mushrooms and cook until they are browned and tender, about 5-7 minutes. Season with a pinch of salt and pepper. Set aside.
3. **Start the Risotto:**
    - In a large pan or Dutch oven, heat the remaining 1 tbsp of olive oil and 1 tbsp of butter over medium heat. Add the chopped onion and cook until softened, about 3-4 minutes.
    - Add the minced garlic and cook for an additional minute.
4. **Add the Rice:**
    - Stir in the Arborio rice and cook, stirring constantly, for 2 minutes until the rice is lightly toasted and coated with oil.
5. **Deglaze with Wine:**
    - Pour in the white wine and cook, stirring constantly, until the wine is mostly absorbed.
6. **Add the Broth:**
    - Begin adding the warm broth to the rice, one ladleful at a time, stirring frequently. Wait until most of the liquid is absorbed before adding the next ladleful. Continue this process until the rice is creamy and cooked to al dente, about 18-20 minutes.
7. **Finish the Risotto:**
    - Stir in the cooked mushrooms, remaining 1 tbsp of butter, and grated Parmesan cheese. Adjust seasoning with salt and pepper. Stir until well combined and creamy.
8. **Serve:**

- Garnish with chopped fresh parsley. Serve hot.

Tips:

- **Mushroom Variety:** Using a mix of wild mushrooms enhances the flavor complexity of the dish.
- **Creaminess:** The key to a creamy risotto is to stir continuously and add the broth gradually.

Wild Mushroom Risotto is a decadent and comforting dish that highlights the earthy flavors of mushrooms combined with the creamy richness of Arborio rice.

Beef Stroganoff

Ingredients:

- 1 lb beef sirloin or tenderloin, thinly sliced into strips
- 2 tbsp olive oil
- 1 medium onion, finely chopped
- 2 garlic cloves, minced
- 1 cup mushrooms, sliced
- 1/2 cup white wine or beef broth
- 1 cup sour cream
- 1 tbsp Dijon mustard
- 2 tbsp all-purpose flour
- 1 cup beef broth
- 1 tbsp Worcestershire sauce
- Salt and freshly ground black pepper, to taste
- 2 tbsp fresh parsley, chopped (for garnish)
- Cooked egg noodles or rice (for serving)

Instructions:

1. **Cook the Beef:**
    - Heat olive oil in a large skillet over medium-high heat. Add the sliced beef and cook until browned on all sides, about 3-4 minutes. Remove the beef from the skillet and set aside.
2. **Sauté the Vegetables:**
    - In the same skillet, add the chopped onion and cook until softened, about 3 minutes. Add the garlic and cook for another minute.
    - Add the sliced mushrooms and cook until they release their juices and are tender, about 5 minutes.
3. **Deglaze the Pan:**
    - Pour in the white wine or beef broth, scraping up any browned bits from the bottom of the skillet. Let it simmer for 2-3 minutes until slightly reduced.
4. **Make the Sauce:**
    - Stir in the flour and cook for 1 minute. Gradually add the beef broth while stirring to avoid lumps. Bring to a simmer and cook until the sauce thickens, about 5 minutes.
5. **Finish the Dish:**
    - Stir in the sour cream, Dijon mustard, and Worcestershire sauce. Return the beef to the skillet and simmer until heated through, about 3-5 minutes. Adjust seasoning with salt and pepper.
6. **Serve:**
    - Garnish with chopped fresh parsley. Serve over cooked egg noodles or rice.

Tips:

- **Beef Tenderness:** For the most tender beef, avoid overcooking and slice against the grain.
- **Creaminess:** To avoid curdling, make sure the sour cream is added off the heat or on very low heat.

Beef Stroganoff is a rich and creamy dish that pairs beautifully with egg noodles or rice, offering a deliciously comforting meal.

Sautéed Foie Gras with Apple Compote

Ingredients:

For the Foie Gras:

- 4 slices of foie gras (about 1/2 inch thick)
- Salt and freshly ground black pepper
- 2 tbsp all-purpose flour (for dusting)
- 1 tbsp olive oil or butter

For the Apple Compote:

- 2 large apples (such as Granny Smith or Honeycrisp), peeled, cored, and diced
- 1/4 cup granulated sugar
- 1/4 cup water
- 1 tbsp lemon juice
- 1/2 tsp ground cinnamon
- 1/4 tsp ground nutmeg
- 1 tbsp unsalted butter

For Garnish:

- Fresh thyme or parsley, chopped (optional)

Instructions:

1. **Prepare the Apple Compote:**
    - In a medium saucepan, combine the diced apples, granulated sugar, water, lemon juice, cinnamon, and nutmeg.
    - Bring to a simmer over medium heat. Cook, stirring occasionally, until the apples are tender and the mixture has thickened, about 10-15 minutes.
    - Stir in the butter and cook for an additional minute until melted and incorporated. Remove from heat and set aside.
2. **Prepare the Foie Gras:**
    - Pat the foie gras slices dry with paper towels. Season with salt and pepper. Lightly dust each slice with flour, shaking off the excess.
    - Heat the olive oil or butter in a non-stick skillet over medium-high heat.
    - Sear the foie gras slices for about 30-45 seconds per side, until golden brown and crispy on the outside but still tender and creamy inside. Be careful not to overcook.
3. **Serve:**
    - Spoon a portion of the apple compote onto each plate.
    - Top with a slice of seared foie gras.
    - Garnish with fresh thyme or parsley if desired.

Tips:

- **Foie Gras Cooking:** Foie gras cooks quickly, so keep an eye on it to avoid overcooking. It should be caramelized on the outside while remaining creamy inside.
- **Compote Variations:** You can add a splash of brandy or a handful of dried fruit (such as raisins) to the compote for extra depth of flavor.

This Sautéed Foie Gras with Apple Compote combines the rich decadence of foie gras with the sweet and spiced apples, making it a sophisticated and elegant dish for a special occasion.

Crab Cakes with Remoulade

Ingredients:

For the Crab Cakes:

- 1 lb fresh lump crab meat, picked over for shells
- 1/2 cup mayonnaise
- 1 large egg
- 2 tbsp Dijon mustard
- 2 tbsp fresh parsley, chopped
- 1/4 cup finely chopped celery
- 1/4 cup finely chopped onion
- 1/4 cup finely chopped red bell pepper
- 1/2 cup panko breadcrumbs (plus extra for coating)
- 1 tbsp Old Bay seasoning or seafood seasoning
- Salt and freshly ground black pepper, to taste
- 2-3 tbsp vegetable oil (for frying)

For the Remoulade Sauce:

- 1/2 cup mayonnaise
- 2 tbsp Dijon mustard
- 1 tbsp lemon juice
- 1 tbsp capers, finely chopped
- 1 tbsp fresh parsley, chopped
- 1 garlic clove, minced
- 1/2 tsp hot sauce (optional)
- Salt and freshly ground black pepper, to taste

Instructions:

1. **Prepare the Crab Cakes:**
    - In a large bowl, gently mix together the crab meat, mayonnaise, egg, Dijon mustard, parsley, celery, onion, red bell pepper, panko breadcrumbs, Old Bay seasoning, salt, and pepper. Be careful not to break up the crab meat too much.
    - Form the mixture into 8-10 patties, about 1/2 to 3/4 inch thick. Coat each patty with additional panko breadcrumbs for a crispy exterior.
    - Place the patties on a baking sheet and refrigerate for at least 30 minutes to help them hold their shape during cooking.
2. **Prepare the Remoulade Sauce:**
    - In a medium bowl, whisk together mayonnaise, Dijon mustard, lemon juice, capers, parsley, garlic, and hot sauce (if using). Season with salt and pepper to taste. Refrigerate until ready to serve.

3. **Cook the Crab Cakes:**
     - Heat vegetable oil in a large skillet over medium heat. Fry the crab cakes in batches, being careful not to overcrowd the pan. Cook for about 3-4 minutes per side, or until golden brown and crisp.
     - Remove from the skillet and drain on paper towels.
4. **Serve:**
     - Serve the crab cakes warm, with a dollop of remoulade sauce on top or on the side.

Tips:

- **Crab Meat:** Use high-quality fresh crab meat for the best flavor. If using canned or frozen crab meat, be sure to drain and thoroughly pick over it.
- **Binding:** If the mixture feels too loose, add more breadcrumbs. If it's too dry, add a bit more mayonnaise.

These Crab Cakes with Remoulade are perfect for a special meal or as a sophisticated appetizer, combining tender crab with a creamy, tangy sauce.

Pan-Roasted Veal Chop

Ingredients:

- 2 veal chops (about 1 1/2 to 2 inches thick)
- Salt and freshly ground black pepper
- 2 tbsp olive oil
- 2 tbsp unsalted butter
- 2 cloves garlic, minced
- 2 sprigs fresh rosemary or thyme (or 1 tsp dried)
- 1/2 cup dry white wine
- 1/2 cup beef or veal broth
- 1 tbsp Dijon mustard
- 1 tbsp fresh parsley, chopped (for garnish)

Instructions:

1. **Prepare the Veal Chops:**
   - Season the veal chops generously with salt and pepper on both sides.
2. **Sear the Veal Chops:**
   - Heat the olive oil in an oven-safe skillet over medium-high heat.
   - When the oil is hot but not smoking, add the veal chops and sear for about 3-4 minutes per side, or until a golden brown crust forms.
3. **Add Butter and Herbs:**
   - Add the butter, garlic, and rosemary or thyme to the skillet. Once the butter is melted, spoon it over the veal chops while they cook for another 1-2 minutes.
4. **Roast the Veal Chops:**
   - Transfer the skillet to a preheated oven at 375°F (190°C).
   - Roast for about 10-12 minutes, or until the veal chops reach your desired level of doneness (135°F/57°C for medium-rare).
5. **Rest the Veal Chops:**
   - Remove the skillet from the oven and transfer the veal chops to a plate. Let them rest for about 5 minutes before slicing.
6. **Make the Pan Sauce:**
   - Place the skillet back on the stovetop over medium heat.
   - Add the white wine to deglaze the pan, scraping up any browned bits with a wooden spoon.
   - Stir in the beef or veal broth and Dijon mustard. Cook until the sauce is reduced and slightly thickened, about 5 minutes.
7. **Serve:**
   - Spoon the pan sauce over the veal chops.
   - Garnish with fresh parsley.

Tips:

- **Doneness:** Use a meat thermometer to ensure the veal is cooked to your liking. Avoid overcooking as veal is best enjoyed medium-rare to medium.
- **Deglazing:** Be sure to scrape up all the flavorful bits from the bottom of the pan to enhance the sauce.

Pan-Roasted Veal Chops are a sophisticated and delectable choice for a special occasion or a luxurious dinner, offering a perfect balance of tender meat and rich, savory sauce.

Stuffed Poblano Peppers

Ingredients:

- 4 large poblano peppers
- 1/2 lb ground beef or ground turkey
- 1/2 cup onion, finely chopped
- 2 cloves garlic, minced
- 1 cup cooked rice (white or brown)
- 1/2 cup corn kernels (fresh, frozen, or canned)
- 1/2 cup black beans, drained and rinsed
- 1/2 cup shredded cheese (cheddar, Monterey Jack, or a blend)
- 1/2 cup tomato sauce
- 1 tsp ground cumin
- 1/2 tsp smoked paprika
- 1/2 tsp chili powder
- Salt and freshly ground black pepper, to taste
- 2 tbsp olive oil
- 1/4 cup fresh cilantro, chopped (for garnish)

Instructions:

1. **Prepare the Peppers:**
   - Preheat the oven to 375°F (190°C).
   - Cut the tops off the poblano peppers and remove the seeds and membranes. Set aside.
2. **Cook the Filling:**
   - Heat olive oil in a large skillet over medium heat. Add the chopped onion and cook until softened, about 3-4 minutes.
   - Add the garlic and cook for another minute.
   - Add the ground beef or turkey and cook until browned. Drain excess fat if necessary.
   - Stir in the cooked rice, corn, black beans, cheese, tomato sauce, cumin, smoked paprika, chili powder, salt, and pepper. Cook until heated through and the cheese is melted.
3. **Stuff the Peppers:**
   - Spoon the filling into each poblano pepper, packing it in gently.
4. **Bake the Peppers:**
   - Place the stuffed peppers in a baking dish. Cover with foil and bake for 25 minutes.
   - Remove the foil and bake for an additional 10 minutes, or until the peppers are tender and the tops are slightly crispy.
5. **Serve:**
   - Garnish with chopped fresh cilantro before serving.

Tips:

- **Pepper Preparation:** If you prefer a softer pepper, you can pre-roast the peppers for 10 minutes before stuffing them.
- **Filling Variations:** Feel free to add or substitute ingredients such as diced tomatoes, chopped spinach, or different types of cheese.

Stuffed Poblano Peppers are a versatile and satisfying dish, combining the smoky flavor of poblanos with a hearty and cheesy filling for a delicious meal.

Sweetbreads with Capers

Ingredients:

- 1 lb sweetbreads (veal or lamb), cleaned and trimmed
- 1 cup milk
- 1/2 cup all-purpose flour
- 2 tbsp olive oil
- 2 tbsp unsalted butter
- 1 small onion, finely chopped
- 2 cloves garlic, minced
- 1/4 cup white wine
- 1/2 cup chicken or veal broth
- 2 tbsp capers, drained and rinsed
- 1 tbsp fresh lemon juice
- 1 tbsp fresh parsley, chopped (for garnish)
- Salt and freshly ground black pepper, to taste

Instructions:

1. **Prepare the Sweetbreads:**
   - Place the sweetbreads in a bowl with milk and refrigerate for at least 2 hours or overnight to soak and tenderize.
2. **Clean and Prep:**
   - After soaking, rinse the sweetbreads and pat them dry. Remove any remaining membranes or connective tissue.
3. **Dredge the Sweetbreads:**
   - Lightly season the sweetbreads with salt and pepper, then dredge them in flour, shaking off the excess.
4. **Sear the Sweetbreads:**
   - Heat olive oil and butter in a large skillet over medium-high heat. Add the sweetbreads and cook until golden brown and crispy on all sides, about 4-5 minutes per side. Remove and set aside.
5. **Make the Sauce:**
   - In the same skillet, add the chopped onion and cook until softened, about 3 minutes. Add the garlic and cook for another minute.
   - Deglaze the pan with white wine, scraping up any browned bits from the bottom. Cook until the wine is reduced by half.
   - Stir in the chicken or veal broth and bring to a simmer. Cook for about 5 minutes, or until the sauce is slightly reduced.
6. **Finish the Dish:**
   - Add the capers and lemon juice to the sauce, stirring to combine. Return the sweetbreads to the skillet and cook for an additional 2-3 minutes, ensuring they are heated through and coated with the sauce.

7. **Serve:**
    - Garnish with chopped fresh parsley. Serve hot, ideally with a side of sautéed vegetables or over a bed of rice or mashed potatoes.

Tips:

- **Cleaning Sweetbreads:** Ensure sweetbreads are well-cleaned and soaked to remove any bitterness.
- **Sauce Reduction:** Adjust the sauce thickness by cooking it longer or adding a bit more broth if needed.

Sweetbreads with Capers is an elegant dish that features tender sweetbreads enhanced by a bright, flavorful sauce, making it a sophisticated choice for a special meal.

Ahi Tuna with Soy Ginger Glaze

Ingredients:

For the Soy Ginger Glaze:

- 1/4 cup soy sauce
- 2 tbsp honey
- 1 tbsp rice vinegar
- 1 tbsp freshly grated ginger
- 2 cloves garlic, minced
- 1 tsp sesame oil
- 1 tbsp cornstarch mixed with 2 tbsp water (optional, for thickening)

For the Tuna:

- 4 ahi tuna steaks (about 6 oz each)
- Salt and freshly ground black pepper, to taste
- 2 tbsp vegetable oil
- 1 tbsp sesame seeds (optional, for garnish)
- 2 green onions, sliced (for garnish)

Instructions:

1. **Prepare the Soy Ginger Glaze:**
    - In a small saucepan, combine soy sauce, honey, rice vinegar, grated ginger, garlic, and sesame oil.
    - Bring to a simmer over medium heat, stirring occasionally.
    - If you prefer a thicker glaze, stir in the cornstarch mixture and cook until the sauce thickens to your desired consistency. Remove from heat and set aside.
2. **Prepare the Tuna Steaks:**
    - Season the ahi tuna steaks with salt and pepper on both sides.
    - Heat vegetable oil in a large skillet or grill pan over medium-high heat.
3. **Sear the Tuna:**
    - Add the tuna steaks to the hot skillet. Sear for about 1-2 minutes on each side for rare (1 minute per side) to medium-rare (2 minutes per side). Adjust the cooking time if you prefer your tuna cooked more or less.
    - Remove the tuna steaks from the skillet and let them rest for a minute or two.
4. **Serve:**
    - Slice the tuna steaks into thick slices.
    - Drizzle the soy ginger glaze over the tuna or serve it on the side.
    - Garnish with sesame seeds and sliced green onions.

Tips:

- **Tuna Quality:** Use high-quality, sushi-grade ahi tuna for the best flavor and texture.
- **Seared Tuna:** Tuna is best served rare to medium-rare. Overcooking can make it dry.

Ahi Tuna with Soy Ginger Glaze offers a deliciously fresh and flavorful meal, perfect for a special dinner or a refined dish for entertaining.

Beef Carpaccio

Ingredients:

- 1 lb beef tenderloin or sirloin, trimmed
- 2 tbsp olive oil
- 1 tbsp lemon juice
- 1 tbsp Dijon mustard
- 1 clove garlic, minced
- 2 tbsp capers, drained
- 1/4 cup shaved Parmesan cheese
- 1/4 cup fresh arugula or baby spinach
- Salt and freshly ground black pepper, to taste
- 1 tbsp fresh parsley, chopped (for garnish)
- Lemon wedges (for serving)

Instructions:

1. **Prepare the Beef:**
    - Place the beef in the freezer for about 30 minutes to firm it up, making it easier to slice thinly.
    - Using a sharp knife, slice the beef as thinly as possible. Arrange the slices in a single layer on a large plate or platter.
2. **Make the Dressing:**
    - In a small bowl, whisk together olive oil, lemon juice, Dijon mustard, minced garlic, salt, and pepper.
3. **Assemble the Carpaccio:**
    - Brush or drizzle the dressing evenly over the sliced beef.
    - Scatter capers over the top.
    - Garnish with shaved Parmesan cheese and fresh arugula or baby spinach.
    - Sprinkle with additional salt, pepper, and fresh parsley.
4. **Serve:**
    - Serve immediately with lemon wedges on the side.

Tips:

- **Beef Quality:** Use high-quality, fresh beef and ensure it's been properly chilled for safe consumption.
- **Slicing:** For even and thin slices, use a sharp knife and slice against the grain.

Beef Carpaccio is a refined and flavorful appetizer, offering a delicate taste of raw beef complemented by tangy and savory elements.

Seafood Paella

Ingredients:

- 2 tbsp olive oil
- 1 onion, finely chopped
- 1 bell pepper, chopped
- 3 cloves garlic, minced
- 1 cup tomatoes, diced (or 1 can diced tomatoes)
- 1 1/2 cups short-grain or paella rice (such as Bomba or Arborio)
- 1/2 tsp saffron threads
- 1 tsp smoked paprika
- 1/2 tsp turmeric (optional, for extra color)
- 4 cups chicken or seafood broth
- 1/2 cup white wine
- 1 cup green peas (fresh or frozen)
- 1 cup cooked shrimp (peeled and deveined)
- 1 cup mussels (cleaned and debearded)
- 1 cup clams (cleaned and scrubbed)
- 1/2 cup squid rings (optional)
- 1 lemon, cut into wedges (for garnish)
- Fresh parsley, chopped (for garnish)
- Salt and freshly ground black pepper, to taste

Instructions:

1. **Prepare the Base:**
   - Heat olive oil in a large paella pan or deep skillet over medium heat.
   - Add the chopped onion and bell pepper. Cook until softened, about 5 minutes.
   - Add the garlic and cook for an additional minute.
2. **Add Tomatoes and Spices:**
   - Stir in the diced tomatoes, saffron, smoked paprika, and turmeric. Cook for 5 minutes until the tomatoes break down and the mixture becomes fragrant.
3. **Add Rice and Liquid:**
   - Add the rice and stir to coat it with the tomato mixture.
   - Pour in the white wine and cook until mostly evaporated.
   - Add the broth, bring to a boil, then reduce heat to low. Simmer for 10-15 minutes without stirring, until the rice is nearly cooked and the liquid is absorbed.
4. **Add Seafood:**
   - Arrange the shrimp, mussels, clams, and squid on top of the rice. Cover and cook for an additional 5-10 minutes, or until the seafood is cooked and the mussels and clams have opened. Discard any that remain closed.
5. **Finish and Serve:**
   - Remove the paella from heat and let it sit for a few minutes.

- Garnish with lemon wedges and fresh parsley.

Tips:

- **Seafood Quality:** Use fresh, high-quality seafood for the best flavor.
- **Rice:** Avoid stirring the rice after adding the broth to develop the traditional socarrat (crispy bottom layer).

Seafood Paella is a vibrant and flavorful dish that brings together a variety of seafood with aromatic spices and tender rice, making it perfect for a festive meal or special occasion.

Tuna Poke Bowl

Ingredients:

For the Tuna Marinade:

- 1 lb (450g) sushi-grade tuna, diced into bite-sized cubes
- 1/4 cup soy sauce
- 1 tbsp sesame oil
- 1 tbsp rice vinegar
- 1 tsp honey or sugar
- 1 tsp grated ginger
- 1 garlic clove, minced
- 1/2 tsp red pepper flakes (optional, for a bit of heat)

For the Bowl:

- 2 cups cooked sushi rice (or any short-grain rice)
- 1 avocado, sliced
- 1 cucumber, thinly sliced
- 1 small carrot, julienned
- 1 radish, thinly sliced
- 1/2 cup edamame (cooked)
- 1/4 cup seaweed salad
- 1/4 cup pickled ginger
- 1-2 tbsp sesame seeds
- 2 green onions, chopped
- Soy sauce or additional ponzu sauce for drizzling

Instructions:

1. **Prepare the Tuna:**
    - In a bowl, combine the soy sauce, sesame oil, rice vinegar, honey, ginger, garlic, and red pepper flakes.
    - Add the diced tuna to the marinade and gently toss to coat. Let it marinate in the refrigerator for about 15-30 minutes.
2. **Prepare the Rice:**
    - Cook the sushi rice according to package instructions. Let it cool slightly before using it as a base for the bowl.
3. **Assemble the Bowl:**
    - Divide the cooked rice between bowls.
    - Arrange the marinated tuna over the rice.
    - Top with avocado slices, cucumber, carrot, radish, edamame, seaweed salad, and pickled ginger.

4. **Garnish and Serve:**
    - Sprinkle sesame seeds and chopped green onions over the top.
    - Drizzle with additional soy sauce or ponzu sauce if desired.

Feel free to adjust the toppings and ingredients based on your preferences or what you have on hand. Enjoy your homemade Tuna Poke Bowl!

Roasted Cornish Hen

Ingredients:

- 2 Cornish hens (about 1 to 1.5 lbs each)
- 2 tbsp olive oil or melted butter
- 4 cloves garlic, minced
- 1 lemon, quartered
- 1 sprig of rosemary
- 1 sprig of thyme
- 1 tsp paprika
- 1 tsp dried oregano
- 1 tsp dried thyme (or 2 tsp fresh thyme)
- Salt and freshly ground black pepper
- 1/2 cup chicken broth (or white wine)

Instructions:

1. **Preheat Oven:**
    - Preheat your oven to 425°F (220°C).
2. **Prepare the Hens:**
    - Remove any giblets from the hens if they're included, and pat the hens dry with paper towels.
    - Rub the outside and inside of each hen with olive oil or melted butter.
3. **Season:**
    - Season the hens generously inside and out with salt and pepper.
    - Rub minced garlic all over the hens.
    - Sprinkle paprika, oregano, and thyme over the hens.
    - Stuff the cavity of each hen with lemon quarters and a sprig each of rosemary and thyme.
4. **Truss the Hens (optional):**
    - To ensure even cooking and a nice presentation, you can truss the hens by tying the legs together with kitchen twine and tucking the wing tips under the body.
5. **Roast:**
    - Place the hens breast side up on a rack in a roasting pan. You can also place them on a bed of vegetables like carrots, onions, and celery for added flavor.
    - Pour the chicken broth (or white wine) into the bottom of the roasting pan.
    - Roast in the preheated oven for about 50-60 minutes, or until the hens are golden brown and the internal temperature reaches 165°F (74°C) when checked at the thickest part of the thigh.
6. **Rest:**
    - Remove the hens from the oven and let them rest for 10-15 minutes before carving. This allows the juices to redistribute and keeps the meat moist.

7. **Serve:**
    - Carve and serve the Cornish hens with your favorite sides. The roasted hens are delicious with roasted vegetables, potatoes, or a fresh salad.

Enjoy your flavorful and succulent roasted Cornish hen!

Miso-Glazed Black Cod

Ingredients:

For the Miso Glaze:

- 1/4 cup white miso paste
- 1/4 cup sake (or dry white wine)
- 1/4 cup mirin (or a mix of 1/4 cup white wine and 1 tablespoon sugar)
- 2 tablespoons sugar
- 1 tablespoon soy sauce

For the Black Cod:

- 4 black cod fillets (about 6 oz each)
- 1 tablespoon vegetable oil

Garnishes (optional):

- Sliced green onions
- Sesame seeds
- Pickled ginger
- Steamed rice

Instructions:

1. **Prepare the Miso Glaze:**
   - In a small saucepan, combine the white miso paste, sake, mirin, sugar, and soy sauce.
   - Heat over medium heat, whisking continuously until the mixture is smooth and the sugar has dissolved. This should take about 3-4 minutes. Remove from heat and let it cool to room temperature.
2. **Marinate the Cod:**
   - Pat the black cod fillets dry with paper towels.
   - Place the fillets in a resealable plastic bag or a shallow dish.
   - Pour half of the cooled miso glaze over the fillets, ensuring they are well coated.
   - Seal the bag or cover the dish and refrigerate for at least 1 hour, or up to 24 hours for more intense flavor.
3. **Preheat the Oven:**
   - Preheat your oven to 400°F (200°C).
4. **Cook the Cod:**
   - Remove the cod from the marinade and discard the used marinade.
   - Brush a baking dish with vegetable oil or line it with parchment paper.
   - Place the fillets in the baking dish, skin side down.

- Bake in the preheated oven for about 12-15 minutes, or until the fish is opaque and flakes easily with a fork. The cod should be caramelized on top from the miso glaze.
5. **Finish with Glaze:**
    - If desired, you can brush the remaining miso glaze over the fillets during the last 5 minutes of baking for an extra layer of flavor and a glossy finish.
6. **Serve:**
    - Garnish with sliced green onions, sesame seeds, and pickled ginger if desired.
    - Serve with steamed rice and your favorite vegetables or a fresh salad.

Enjoy your beautifully glazed black cod!

Grilled Lobster Tail

Ingredients:

- 4 lobster tails (about 6-8 oz each)
- 1/4 cup melted butter (or olive oil)
- 2 cloves garlic, minced
- 1 lemon, juiced
- 1 teaspoon paprika
- 1 teaspoon dried oregano or thyme
- Salt and freshly ground black pepper
- Fresh parsley, chopped (for garnish)
- Lemon wedges (for serving)

Instructions:

1. **Prepare the Lobster Tails:**
   - Using kitchen shears or a sharp knife, cut along the top of the lobster tail shell, from the base to the tip, but don't cut all the way through.
   - Gently pry open the shell and loosen the lobster meat from the shell, leaving it attached at the base. You can also lift the meat slightly above the shell for an easier presentation.
2. **Preheat the Grill:**
   - Preheat your grill to medium-high heat, around 375°F to 400°F (190°C to 200°C). You can use a gas or charcoal grill.
3. **Prepare the Butter Mixture:**
   - In a small bowl, combine the melted butter, minced garlic, lemon juice, paprika, dried oregano (or thyme), salt, and pepper.
4. **Season the Lobster:**
   - Brush the lobster meat generously with the butter mixture.
5. **Grill the Lobster:**
   - Place the lobster tails flesh side down on the grill. Close the lid and cook for about 4-6 minutes.
   - Flip the lobster tails over and brush again with the butter mixture. Continue grilling for another 4-6 minutes, or until the lobster meat is opaque and easily flakes with a fork. The internal temperature should reach 140°F (60°C).
6. **Finish and Serve:**
   - Remove the lobster tails from the grill and brush with any remaining butter mixture.
   - Garnish with chopped fresh parsley and serve with lemon wedges on the side.

Tips:

- **Don't Overcook:** Lobster cooks quickly and can become tough if overcooked. Keep an eye on it and use a meat thermometer to ensure it reaches the right temperature.
- **Grill Marks:** For nice grill marks, make sure the grill grates are clean and preheated. Avoid moving the lobster tails too much once they're on the grill.

Grilled lobster tails are perfect for a special occasion or a luxurious treat. Enjoy them with a side of grilled vegetables, a fresh salad, or some buttery garlic bread!

Braised Lamb Shanks

Ingredients:

- 4 lamb shanks (about 1.5 lbs each)
- Salt and freshly ground black pepper
- 2 tbsp olive oil
- 1 onion, chopped
- 2 carrots, chopped
- 2 celery stalks, chopped
- 4 cloves garlic, minced
- 1 cup red wine
- 2 cups beef or chicken broth
- 1 (14.5 oz) can diced tomatoes
- 2 tbsp tomato paste
- 2 sprigs fresh rosemary (or 1 tsp dried rosemary)
- 2 sprigs fresh thyme (or 1 tsp dried thyme)
- 1 bay leaf

Instructions:

1. **Preheat Oven:**
    - Preheat your oven to 325°F (160°C).
2. **Season and Sear:**
    - Season the lamb shanks generously with salt and pepper.
    - In a large Dutch oven or oven-safe pot, heat olive oil over medium-high heat.
    - Sear the lamb shanks on all sides until browned, about 4-5 minutes per side. Remove and set aside.
3. **Sauté Vegetables:**
    - In the same pot, add onions, carrots, and celery. Sauté until softened, about 5 minutes.
    - Add garlic and cook for another minute.
4. **Deglaze:**
    - Pour in the red wine, scraping up any browned bits from the bottom of the pot. Let it simmer for 2-3 minutes until slightly reduced.
5. **Add Liquids and Herbs:**
    - Stir in the beef or chicken broth, diced tomatoes, tomato paste, rosemary, thyme, and bay leaf.
    - Return the lamb shanks to the pot, nestling them into the liquid.
6. **Braise:**
    - Bring the liquid to a simmer, then cover the pot with a lid and transfer it to the preheated oven.
    - Braise for 2.5 to 3 hours, or until the meat is tender and falling off the bone.

7. **Finish:**
    - Remove the lamb shanks from the pot and let them rest for a few minutes. Skim excess fat from the sauce if needed.
    - If the sauce is too thin, you can reduce it on the stovetop by simmering it until it thickens.
8. **Serve:**
    - Serve the lamb shanks with the sauce spooned over the top, alongside mashed potatoes, polenta, or a hearty grain.

Enjoy your flavorful and tender braised lamb shanks!

Butternut Squash Soup

Ingredients:

- 1 large butternut squash (about 2 lbs), peeled, seeded, and cubed
- 2 tbsp olive oil
- 1 onion, chopped
- 2 cloves garlic, minced
- 1 apple, peeled and chopped (optional, for added sweetness)
- 4 cups vegetable or chicken broth
- 1/2 cup coconut milk or heavy cream
- 1 tsp ground cumin
- 1/2 tsp ground nutmeg
- Salt and freshly ground black pepper
- Fresh parsley or cilantro, for garnish

Instructions:

1. **Roast the Squash:**
    - Preheat your oven to 400°F (200°C).
    - Toss the cubed butternut squash with 1 tablespoon of olive oil, salt, and pepper.
    - Spread the squash on a baking sheet in a single layer. Roast for 25-30 minutes, or until tender and caramelized.
2. **Sauté Vegetables:**
    - In a large pot, heat the remaining tablespoon of olive oil over medium heat.
    - Add the chopped onion and cook until softened, about 5 minutes.
    - Add the minced garlic and cook for another minute. If using apple, add it now and cook for 5 minutes.
3. **Combine and Blend:**
    - Add the roasted butternut squash to the pot.
    - Pour in the broth, and bring the mixture to a simmer. Cook for 10 minutes to allow the flavors to meld.
    - Use an immersion blender to blend the soup until smooth. Alternatively, blend in batches using a countertop blender.
4. **Finish and Serve:**
    - Stir in the coconut milk or heavy cream, ground cumin, and nutmeg.
    - Season with salt and pepper to taste.
    - Heat the soup until warmed through, then serve garnished with fresh parsley or cilantro.

Enjoy your creamy and flavorful butternut squash soup!

Pork Belly with Apple Chutney

Ingredients:

For the Pork Belly:

- 2 lbs pork belly, skin-on
- Salt
- Black pepper
- 2 tbsp olive oil

For the Apple Chutney:

- 2 tbsp olive oil
- 1 onion, finely chopped
- 2 cloves garlic, minced
- 2 apples, peeled, cored, and chopped (e.g., Granny Smith or Honeycrisp)
- 1/2 cup brown sugar
- 1/2 cup apple cider vinegar
- 1/2 cup raisins or dried cranberries
- 1/2 tsp ground ginger
- 1/2 tsp ground cinnamon
- 1/4 tsp ground cloves
- Salt and pepper to taste

Instructions:

1. **Prepare the Pork Belly:**
    - Preheat your oven to 300°F (150°C).
    - Pat the pork belly dry with paper towels. Score the skin in a crisscross pattern, being careful not to cut into the meat.
    - Rub the pork belly generously with salt and black pepper, making sure it gets into the scored skin.
    - Place the pork belly on a rack in a roasting pan, skin side up. Drizzle with olive oil.
    - Roast in the preheated oven for 2.5 to 3 hours, or until the meat is tender and the skin is crispy. You may need to increase the temperature to 400°F (200°C) for the last 30 minutes to get the skin extra crispy.
2. **Prepare the Apple Chutney:**
    - While the pork belly is roasting, heat olive oil in a saucepan over medium heat.
    - Add the chopped onion and cook until softened and translucent, about 5 minutes.
    - Add the garlic and cook for another minute.
    - Stir in the chopped apples, brown sugar, apple cider vinegar, raisins (or dried cranberries), ground ginger, cinnamon, and cloves.

- Bring to a simmer and cook for 20-25 minutes, or until the apples are tender and the chutney has thickened. Stir occasionally.
- Season with salt and pepper to taste. Let the chutney cool slightly.

3. **Serve:**
   - Once the pork belly is done, remove it from the oven and let it rest for 10 minutes before slicing.
   - Serve the pork belly slices with a generous spoonful of apple chutney on the side.

Tips:

- **Resting the Meat:** Let the pork belly rest after roasting to ensure it remains juicy.
- **Crispy Skin:** For extra crispy skin, you can place the pork belly under the broiler for a few minutes, but watch it closely to prevent burning.
- **Make Ahead:** Both the pork belly and apple chutney can be made ahead of time. Reheat gently before serving.

Enjoy your flavorful pork belly with the sweet and tangy apple chutney!

Crispy Duck Breast

Ingredients:

- 2 duck breasts (about 6-8 oz each)
- Salt
- Black pepper
- 1 tsp dried thyme or rosemary (optional)
- 1 tbsp vegetable oil

For the Glaze (optional):

- 1/4 cup honey
- 2 tbsp soy sauce
- 1 tbsp balsamic vinegar

Instructions:

1. **Prepare the Duck Breasts:**
   - Pat the duck breasts dry with paper towels.
   - Using a sharp knife, score the skin of each duck breast in a crosshatch pattern, being careful not to cut into the meat. This helps render the fat and crisp up the skin.
   - Season both sides of the duck breasts generously with salt, black pepper, and dried thyme or rosemary if using.
2. **Cook the Duck Breasts:**
   - Heat a skillet over medium heat. Add the vegetable oil.
   - Place the duck breasts skin-side down in the skillet. You should hear a sizzle. Cook for about 6-8 minutes, or until the skin is crispy and golden brown. You may need to adjust the heat to prevent burning.
   - Flip the duck breasts over and cook for an additional 3-4 minutes, or until the meat is cooked to your desired level of doneness (medium-rare is recommended, with an internal temperature of 135°F or 57°C).
3. **Rest the Duck:**
   - Remove the duck breasts from the skillet and let them rest on a cutting board for 5 minutes before slicing. This allows the juices to redistribute.
4. **Prepare the Glaze (optional):**
   - While the duck is resting, you can make a simple glaze if desired.
   - In a small saucepan, combine honey, soy sauce, and balsamic vinegar. Bring to a simmer over medium heat, stirring frequently, until the glaze is slightly thickened, about 5 minutes. Remove from heat.
5. **Serve:**
   - Slice the duck breasts against the grain.

- Drizzle with the honey-soy glaze if using, or serve with your favorite sauce or side dishes.

Tips:

- **Rendering Fat:** Cooking the duck skin-side down first helps render out the fat and ensures a crispy skin. Be patient and don't rush this step.
- **Doneness:** Duck breast is typically served medium-rare, but adjust cooking times if you prefer it more well-done.
- **Resting:** Allowing the duck to rest is crucial for juicy, tender meat.

Enjoy your perfectly crispy duck breast with a delicious sauce or a side of roasted vegetables!

Baked Alaska

Ingredients:

For the Base:

- 1 sponge cake or pound cake, sliced to fit the base of your dessert (store-bought or homemade)

For the Ice Cream:

- 1 quart (1 liter) of ice cream, softened (flavor of your choice, like vanilla, chocolate, or fruit)

For the Meringue:

- 4 large egg whites
- 1/2 tsp cream of tartar
- 1/2 cup granulated sugar
- 1/2 tsp vanilla extract

Instructions:

1. **Prepare the Cake Base:**
    - Preheat your oven to 425°F (220°C).
    - Place a round or oval cake pan on a baking sheet. Line it with plastic wrap or parchment paper.
    - Fit the slices of cake into the bottom and sides of the pan, creating a solid layer. You can use any type of cake that holds its shape well.
2. **Add the Ice Cream:**
    - Scoop softened ice cream into the cake-lined pan. Smooth it out evenly with a spatula.
    - Freeze the assembled base until firm, about 2 hours or more.
3. **Prepare the Meringue:**
    - In a clean, dry bowl, beat the egg whites with cream of tartar using an electric mixer until soft peaks form.
    - Gradually add sugar, a tablespoon at a time, beating until stiff, glossy peaks form. Stir in the vanilla extract.
4. **Assemble and Bake:**
    - Remove the ice cream and cake from the pan, discarding the plastic wrap or parchment paper.
    - Place the ice cream-covered cake onto a baking sheet.

- Spread the meringue over the entire dessert, sealing the edges so no ice cream is visible. Use a spatula to create peaks and swirls in the meringue for a decorative effect.
5. **Bake:**
   - Bake in the preheated oven for 4-6 minutes, or until the meringue is golden brown. Keep a close eye on it to prevent burning.
6. **Serve:**
   - Remove from the oven and serve immediately. Baked Alaska is best enjoyed right after baking while the meringue is crisp and the ice cream is still cold.

Tips:

- **Ice Cream Texture:** Make sure the ice cream is softened enough to spread easily but still firm enough to hold its shape.
- **Meringue:** Beat the egg whites until they form stiff peaks, which helps the meringue hold its shape and create a beautiful crust.

Enjoy your elegant and delicious Baked Alaska!

Chocolate Fondant

Ingredients:

- 1/2 cup (1 stick) unsalted butter
- 4 oz (113g) high-quality dark chocolate (60-70% cocoa), chopped
- 1 cup powdered sugar
- 2 large eggs
- 2 large egg yolks
- 1/2 tsp vanilla extract
- 1/2 cup all-purpose flour
- Pinch of salt
- Butter and cocoa powder (for greasing ramekins)

Instructions:

1. **Preheat Oven:**
   - Preheat your oven to 425°F (220°C).
2. **Prepare Ramekins:**
   - Butter four ramekins and dust them with cocoa powder, tapping out any excess. This helps prevent sticking.
3. **Melt Butter and Chocolate:**
   - In a microwave-safe bowl or using a double boiler, melt the butter and chopped dark chocolate together. Stir until smooth and let it cool slightly.
4. **Mix Batter:**
   - In a separate bowl, whisk together the powdered sugar, eggs, egg yolks, and vanilla extract until well combined.
   - Fold in the melted chocolate mixture until fully incorporated.
   - Gently fold in the flour and a pinch of salt until the batter is smooth and well-mixed.
5. **Fill Ramekins:**
   - Divide the batter evenly among the prepared ramekins.
6. **Bake:**
   - Bake in the preheated oven for 12-14 minutes, or until the edges are set but the centers are still soft and jiggly. The tops should look slightly domed and cracked.
7. **Serve:**
   - Let the fondants cool in the ramekins for 1 minute. Run a knife around the edges to loosen them.
   - Invert each ramekin onto a plate and gently lift it off. The fondant should come out easily with a gooey center.

Tips:

- **Timing:** Be careful not to overbake the fondants; the center should remain molten. If you're unsure, you can test one with a toothpick inserted into the center. It should come out with a bit of gooey chocolate on it.
- **Preparation:** You can prepare the batter in advance and refrigerate it. Just bring it back to room temperature before baking.

Optional Serving Suggestions:

- **Ice Cream:** Serve with a scoop of vanilla or coffee ice cream.
- **Fruit:** Fresh berries or a berry sauce add a nice contrast.
- **Whipped Cream:** A dollop of whipped cream is a classic complement.

Enjoy your rich and gooey chocolate fondant!Get smarter responses, upload files and images, and more.

Classic Tiramisu

Ingredients:

- **For the Coffee Mixture:**
    - 1 cup strong brewed coffee, cooled
    - 1/4 cup coffee liqueur (e.g., Marsala wine, Kahlua, or optional)
- **For the Mascarpone Cream:**
    - 6 large egg yolks
    - 3/4 cup granulated sugar
    - 1 cup heavy cream
    - 8 oz (225g) mascarpone cheese, softened
    - 1 tsp vanilla extract
- **For Assembly:**
    - 24-30 ladyfingers (savoiardi)
    - Unsweetened cocoa powder (for dusting)
    - Optional: grated dark chocolate for garnish

Instructions:

1. **Prepare the Coffee Mixture:**
    - In a shallow dish, combine the brewed coffee and coffee liqueur. Set aside.
2. **Make the Mascarpone Cream:**
    - In a large bowl, whisk egg yolks and sugar together until pale and thick.
    - Place the bowl over a pot of simmering water (double boiler) and whisk constantly for about 5 minutes until the mixture is warm but not hot. Remove from heat and let it cool slightly.
    - In a separate bowl, whip the heavy cream until stiff peaks form.
    - Fold the mascarpone cheese and vanilla extract into the egg yolk mixture until smooth.
    - Gently fold the whipped cream into the mascarpone mixture until fully combined.
3. **Assemble the Tiramisu:**
    - Briefly dip each ladyfinger into the coffee mixture, making sure not to soak them.
    - Arrange a layer of dipped ladyfingers in the bottom of a 9x13-inch dish or a similar-sized trifle dish.
    - Spread half of the mascarpone cream mixture over the ladyfingers.
    - Add another layer of dipped ladyfingers and top with the remaining mascarpone cream.
4. **Chill:**
    - Cover and refrigerate the tiramisu for at least 4 hours, preferably overnight, to allow the flavors to meld and the dessert to set properly.
5. **Serve:**

- Before serving, dust the top with unsweetened cocoa powder. Optionally, sprinkle with grated dark chocolate.

Tips:

- **Coffee:** Use strong coffee for a more robust flavor. Adjust the coffee liqueur to taste or omit it if preferred.
- **Egg Safety:** Ensure that the egg yolks are cooked in the double boiler to reduce any risk of raw egg consumption.

Enjoy your classic, creamy tiramisu!

www.ingramcontent.com/pod-product-compliance
Lightning Source LLC
LaVergne TN
LVHW081603060526
838201LV00054B/2047